The Essential Bread Machine Cookbook for Beginners

The Ultimate Guide with Delicious, Easy & Quick Bread Making Recipes with Step-By-Step Instructions. Includes Gluten-Free, Keto and Vegan Options.

JULIA SMITH

Summary

Chapter 1: Introduction to Baking with a Bread Machine

1.1 What is a Bread Machine?

A bread machine is an invaluable kitchen appliance designed to make the process of baking bread both effortless and enjoyable. This versatile device combines several key functions into one compact unit, transforming raw ingredients into a freshly baked loaf with minimal intervention. Understanding the bread machine's core functions, variations in models, and advantages over traditional bread-making methods can help you make the most of this handy tool.

Overview of the Bread Machine and Its Main Functions

At its core, a bread machine simplifies the bread-making process by automating several crucial steps. The appliance is designed to mix, knead, rise, and bake the dough all in one place, which greatly reduces the hands-on time and effort typically involved in baking bread from scratch.

The bread-making journey starts with the mixing process. When you add your ingredients to the machine's pan, the appliance uses a kneading blade or paddle to thoroughly combine them. This initial stage is crucial because it ensures that all ingredients, from flour and yeast to water and salt, are evenly distributed. Proper mixing lays the foundation for a well-structured dough.

Following mixing, the machine proceeds to the kneading phase. This step is essential for developing the gluten in the flour, which gives bread its chewy texture and airy structure. During kneading, the machine's paddle works to fold and stretch the dough, integrating air and promoting the formation of gluten networks. This phase typically lasts between 10 and 20 minutes, depending on the machine and the recipe.

Once kneading is complete, the dough must rise, or proof. The bread machine takes over this task by maintaining an optimal environment for yeast to grow. The internal temperature and humidity are carefully regulated, allowing the dough to double in size as the yeast ferments and produces carbon dioxide. This rising phase is crucial for achieving a light and fluffy loaf.

The final stage in the bread-making process is baking. The machine switches to a baking mode where a built-in heating element evenly cooks the dough. The result is a beautifully browned crust and a soft, flavorful interior. Most bread machines feature different baking options, such as light or dark crust settings, to cater to personal preferences.

Differences Between Various Bread Machine Models

Bread machines come in a range of models, each offering unique features and functionalities. Understanding these differences can help you select the model that best suits your needs and preferences.

Basic bread machines are designed to handle the fundamental tasks of mixing, kneading, rising, and baking. They are ideal for users who seek simplicity and efficiency without additional frills. These models typically come with standard settings for various types of bread, such as white or whole wheat.

Advanced models, on the other hand, offer a broader array of features. These may include programmable settings that allow you to customize baking times and temperatures according to specific recipes. Some advanced machines also provide pre-set programs for different types of bread, such as French, multigrain, or gluten-free, making it easier to bake a variety of loaves.

Another significant difference among models is the shape and size of the baking pan. Bread machines generally come with either a horizontal or vertical pan. Horizontal pans are more common and produce traditional loaf shapes, which are ideal for making sandwiches. Vertical pans, which are often more compact, are suitable for smaller households or limited kitchen space. The size of the pan affects not only the shape of the loaf but also its volume.

Many modern bread machines feature timers or delay start functions, allowing you to set the machine to begin baking at a later time. This feature is particularly useful if you want to wake up to the smell of fresh bread or have it ready when you return home from work. The ability to program the machine in advance means you can enjoy freshly baked bread at your convenience.

Some bread machines also come with additional functions, such as a built-in fruit and nut dispenser. This feature automatically adds ingredients like nuts, seeds, or dried fruit at the optimal time during the kneading process, ensuring even distribution without the need for manual intervention.

Benefits of Using a Bread Machine Compared to Traditional Bread Making

The bread machine offers numerous benefits over traditional bread-making methods, making it an appealing choice for both novice and experienced bakers alike.

One of the most significant advantages is convenience. A bread machine simplifies the bread-making process by automating many of the labor-intensive steps. With just a few basic actions—adding ingredients and selecting a program—you can enjoy freshly baked bread with minimal effort. This convenience is especially valuable for those with busy schedules who still want to enjoy homemade bread.

Consistency is another key benefit of using a bread machine. The automated process ensures that the dough is mixed, kneaded, and baked uniformly, leading to consistent results with each use. This reliability reduces the likelihood of variations in texture and taste that can occur with manual bread-making methods.

Time-saving is a major advantage as well. Traditional bread-making involves several time-consuming steps, including manual mixing, kneading, and baking. The bread machine streamlines these processes, allowing you to enjoy homemade bread without spending hours in the kitchen.

The flexibility to customize recipes is another benefit of using a bread machine. Many models allow you to experiment with various ingredients and adjust recipes to suit your tastes. Whether you prefer to use whole grain flours, add herbs and spices, or try different types of yeast, a bread machine can accommodate your preferences and help you achieve the perfect loaf.

Reducing physical effort is a significant advantage for those who may have limited strength or mobility. Traditional bread-making often requires substantial manual kneading, which can be physically demanding. The bread machine automates this process, making bread-making accessible to everyone.

Additionally, homemade bread often tastes better and is healthier than store-bought alternatives. By using fresh, high-quality ingredients and avoiding preservatives or artificial additives, you can enjoy bread that is both delicious and nutritious. The ability to control the ingredients and avoid unnecessary additives ensures that you are making a healthier choice for you and your family.

Finally, while there is an initial investment in purchasing a bread machine, making bread at home can be more cost-effective in the long run. High-quality artisan bread from bakeries can be expensive, whereas baking at home allows you to enjoy fresh bread at a lower cost.

In conclusion, the bread machine is a powerful and convenient tool that transforms the process of bread-making. With its ability to mix, knead, rise, and bake with minimal effort, it offers significant advantages over traditional methods. By understanding the functions, variations, and benefits of bread machines, you can make an informed choice and enjoy the satisfaction of freshly baked bread from the comfort of your own home.

1.2 How a Bread Machine Works

Understanding how a bread machine operates is essential for making the most of this powerful kitchen tool. By automating the bread-making process, bread machines simplify what used to be a labor-intensive task. In this section, we'll delve into the automated bread-making process, common settings and their uses, and how to properly prepare and measure ingredients for optimal results.

The Automated Bread-Making Process

A bread machine automates every crucial step of bread-making: mixing, kneading, rising, and baking. This automation not only saves time but also ensures consistent results, making it easier for both beginners and seasoned bakers to achieve perfectly baked bread.

1. Mixing:

When you first add your ingredients to the bread machine's pan, the mixing process begins. The bread machine's kneading blade or paddle plays a crucial role here. It rotates to blend all the ingredients, such as flour, water, yeast, and salt, into a cohesive dough. The mixing phase is vital because it ensures that all components are uniformly distributed. In traditional bread-making, this step requires manual effort, but the bread machine does the hard work for you, saving time and energy.

2. Kneading:

Once the initial mixing is complete, the bread machine transitions to the kneading phase. This is where the dough is repeatedly folded and stretched by the kneading blade. Kneading is essential for developing gluten, the protein network that gives bread its structure and chewy texture. The gluten forms when flour proteins interact with water and are physically manipulated during kneading. The bread machine's consistent and controlled kneading ensures that the dough develops the right texture without the need for manual effort. Most machines knead the dough for 10 to 20 minutes, depending on the recipe and the machine's settings.

3. Rising (Proofing):

After kneading, the dough needs to rise, a process also known as proofing or fermentation. During this phase, the bread machine maintains an optimal temperature and humidity level to allow the yeast to work its magic. Yeast ferments the dough, producing carbon dioxide and alcohol, which causes the dough to expand and become airy. The bread machine provides a controlled environment that ensures even and consistent rising, leading to a light and fluffy loaf. This step is crucial because it affects the final texture and volume of the bread.

4. Baking:

The final stage is baking, where the bread machine switches to its baking mode. The machine's heating element warms the dough evenly, creating a golden-brown crust and cooking the interior to perfection. The baking phase typically lasts between 50 to 70 minutes, depending on the size of the loaf and the specific machine settings. Modern bread machines often come with adjustable crust settings, allowing you to choose between light, medium, or dark crusts based on your preference.

5. Cooling:

Once baking is complete, some bread machines automatically switch to a cooling mode or keep-warm function. This helps prevent the bread from cooling too quickly, which can affect its texture. It's important to follow the manufacturer's instructions for cooling the bread, as removing it too early can lead to a soggy or dense loaf. Ideally, the bread should cool on a wire rack to allow air circulation around all sides.

Common Settings and Their Uses

Bread machines come equipped with various settings that cater to different types of bread and baking needs. Understanding these settings helps you make the most of your machine and achieve the best results.

1. Basic or White Bread Setting:

This setting is designed for standard white bread recipes. It follows a straightforward process of mixing, kneading, rising, and baking, making it ideal for everyday bread. It's a great option for beginners or for those who prefer a simple, no-fuss approach to bread-making.

2. Whole Wheat Setting:

Whole wheat bread requires a longer kneading and rising time due to the denser texture of whole wheat flour. The whole wheat setting on your bread machine adjusts the kneading and rising times to accommodate the unique properties of whole wheat flour, resulting in a denser, more flavorful loaf.

3. French Bread Setting:

French bread has a crispier crust and a lighter, airier interior compared to other types of bread. The French bread setting typically includes a longer baking time and higher baking temperature to achieve the distinctive crust and crumb texture of French bread. It's perfect for those who enjoy a crusty, artisan-style loaf.

4. Dough Setting:

The dough setting is ideal for recipes that require additional shaping or baking outside the bread machine. This setting handles the mixing and kneading of dough but skips the rising and baking stages. You can use it to prepare dough for rolls, pizza, or even cinnamon buns, which you then shape and bake separately.

5. Gluten-Free Setting:

Gluten-free bread requires different handling due to the absence of gluten, which affects the dough's texture and rising ability. The gluten-free setting adjusts the kneading and rising times to accommodate gluten-free flours and ingredients, resulting in a tender, well-risen loaf suitable for those with gluten sensitivities.

6. Quick Bread Setting:

Quick breads, such as banana bread or zucchini bread, use baking powder or baking soda instead of yeast. The quick bread setting adjusts the baking time and temperature to ensure that these non-yeast-based recipes are baked to perfection. This setting is useful for making quick and easy sweet or savory breads.

7. Jam or Cake Setting:

Some bread machines come with additional settings for making jams or cakes. The jam setting is designed for cooking fruit preserves, while the cake setting allows you to bake cakes in the bread machine. These settings expand the versatility of your appliance, enabling you to create a wider variety of homemade treats.

8. Delay Timer:

The delay timer function allows you to set the machine to start baking at a later time. This is useful if you want to have freshly baked bread ready for breakfast or when you return home from work. You can add your ingredients and program the machine to begin the process at a specified time, so you wake up or come home to the delightful aroma of fresh bread.

Preparing and Measuring Ingredients

Proper preparation and measurement of ingredients are crucial for achieving consistent and high-quality results with your bread machine. Accurate measurement ensures that the dough has the right balance of ingredients, which affects the bread's texture, flavor, and rise.

1. Measuring Flour:

When measuring flour, it's important to use a dry measuring cup and a spoon. Fluff the flour in its container, then spoon it into the measuring cup and level it off with a straight edge, such as a knife. This method prevents packing the flour down, which can lead to an excess of flour and a dense loaf. For precise measurement, you can also use a kitchen scale to weigh the flour.

2. Measuring Liquids:

Use a liquid measuring cup for measuring liquids like water, milk, or oil. Place the measuring cup on a flat surface and read the measurement at eye level to ensure accuracy. For recipes requiring warm liquids, such as water or milk, ensure that they are at the appropriate temperature, as specified in the recipe. Too hot or too cold liquids can affect the yeast's activity and the dough's rise.

3. Measuring Yeast:

Yeast is a crucial ingredient in bread-making, and precise measurement is essential for proper dough rise. Use a measuring spoon to measure yeast, and ensure that it is fresh and active. Active dry yeast should be proofed in warm water before adding to the dough, while instant yeast can be mixed directly with dry ingredients.

4. Measuring Salt and Sugar:

Salt and sugar should be measured using measuring spoons. Salt is important for flavor and controlling yeast activity, while sugar provides food for the yeast and contributes to browning. Accurate measurement ensures that the bread has the right balance of flavor and texture.

5. Adding Ingredients in the Correct Order:

Follow the recipe's instructions for the order of adding ingredients to the bread machine. Typically, liquids are added first, followed by dry ingredients and yeast. Adding ingredients in the correct order helps ensure proper mixing and dough development.

6. Handling Special Ingredients:

If your recipe includes special ingredients such as seeds, nuts, or dried fruit, make sure to add them at the appropriate time. Some bread machines have a special dispenser for these additions, while others require manual incorporation during the kneading phase. Adding special ingredients at the right time ensures even distribution and prevents overmixing or burning.

In summary, understanding how a bread machine works—from its automated process to the various settings and ingredient preparation—empowers you to achieve excellent results in your bread-making endeavors. By following these guidelines, you can confidently use your bread machine to create a wide variety of delicious and freshly baked breads.

1.3 Tips for Getting Started

Embarking on the journey of bread-making with a bread machine can be both exciting and daunting. With a little guidance and preparation, you can easily master the art of making delicious, homemade bread. This section will provide you with valuable tips on selecting the right ingredients, preparing them for optimal results, and troubleshooting common issues that may arise during the bread-making process.

Selecting Ingredients: Flours, Yeasts, and Additives

The foundation of great bread begins with the selection of high-quality ingredients. Each component plays a critical role in determining the texture, flavor, and overall success of your bread.

1. Flours:

Flour is the primary ingredient in bread, and choosing the right type is essential for achieving the desired results. There are several types of flour available, each with distinct properties:

- **All-Purpose Flour:** This is the most versatile flour and works well for most bread recipes. It has a moderate protein content, which provides a good balance between tenderness and structure. It's a great starting point for beginners.
- **Bread Flour:** With a higher protein content compared to all-purpose flour, bread flour helps create a stronger gluten structure, resulting in a chewier texture and better rise. This flour is ideal for recipes that require a robust structure, such as artisan breads.
- **Whole Wheat Flour:** Made from the entire grain, whole wheat flour imparts a nutty flavor and dense texture to bread. It requires more liquid than white flour and benefits from longer kneading and rising times. For the best results, you can use a combination of whole wheat and all-purpose flours.
- **Specialty Flours:** For specific recipes or dietary needs, you may encounter specialty flours such as rye, spelt, or oat flour. Each of these flours adds unique flavors and textures to your bread but may require adjustments to the recipe.

2. Yeasts:

Yeast is a living organism that ferments the dough, causing it to rise. Selecting the right type of yeast and ensuring its freshness are crucial for successful bread-making:

- **Active Dry Yeast:** This is the most common type of yeast and needs to be dissolved in warm water before being added to the dough. Make sure to proof the yeast by checking for bubbles or froth in the water to confirm its activity.
- **Instant Yeast:** Also known as rapid-rise or bread machine yeast, this type can be mixed directly with dry ingredients without needing to be proofed. It works quickly and is ideal for bread machines.
- **Fresh Yeast:** This yeast comes in a cake form and must be refrigerated. It has a shorter shelf life and needs to be crumbled and dissolved before use. Fresh yeast can offer a more complex flavor but is less commonly used in bread machines.

3. Additives:

Additives such as salt, sugar, fats, and other flavorings enhance the taste and texture of your bread:

- **Salt:** Salt is essential for flavor and regulating yeast activity. It strengthens gluten and helps control fermentation. Always use the amount specified in the recipe to avoid over or under-seasoning your bread.
- **Sugar:** Sugar provides food for the yeast, helping it to ferment and rise. It also contributes to browning and flavor. Adjust the amount of sugar according to your taste and the sweetness of other ingredients.

- **Fats:** Ingredients like butter, oil, or eggs add richness and moisture to the bread. They improve the texture and shelf life of the bread. Ensure that fats are at room temperature before adding them to the dough.
- **Other Additives:** Ingredients such as seeds, nuts, dried fruits, or herbs can be added for extra flavor and texture. Be mindful of their quantity and the timing of their addition to ensure even distribution.

Preparing Ingredients for the Bread Machine

Proper preparation of ingredients ensures that your bread turns out as expected. Here are some tips for preparing ingredients before adding them to your bread machine:

1. Measuring Ingredients:

Accuracy in measuring ingredients is crucial for successful bread-making. Use dry measuring cups for flour and other dry ingredients, and liquid measuring cups for liquids. For precise measurements, especially with flour, use a kitchen scale. Fluff the flour before spooning it into the measuring cup to avoid packing it down, which can result in too much flour in your dough.

2. Temperature of Liquids:

The temperature of liquids, such as water or milk, can significantly impact yeast activity. Most bread recipes call for warm liquids, around 110°F (43°C). This temperature helps to activate the yeast without killing it. Use a thermometer to ensure the liquid is at the correct temperature, and avoid using hot or cold liquids, as they can disrupt the fermentation process.

3. Mixing Ingredients:

Follow the recipe's instructions for the order in which ingredients should be added to the bread machine. Typically, liquids are added first, followed by dry ingredients and yeast. Adding ingredients in the correct order helps prevent clumping and ensures even mixing. If your recipe includes additional ingredients like seeds or dried fruit, add them at the appropriate time as specified in the recipe.

4. Ingredient Substitutions:

If you need to substitute ingredients due to dietary restrictions or personal preferences, make sure to adjust the recipe accordingly. For example, using a gluten-free flour blend instead of all-purpose flour requires modifications to the recipe's liquid content and rising times. Research and test substitutions in small batches to achieve the desired results.

Common Problems and Quick Fixes

Even with the best preparation, issues can arise during the bread-making process. Here are some common problems and quick fixes to help you troubleshoot:

1. Dense or Heavy Bread:

If your bread turns out dense or heavy, it could be due to several factors:

- **Too Much Flour:** Excess flour can make the dough too stiff and prevent proper rising. Ensure that you measure flour accurately and use the spoon-and-level method or a kitchen scale.
- **Insufficient Kneading:** If the dough was not kneaded enough, it may lack the necessary gluten structure. Check your machine's kneading cycle and ensure it's functioning correctly.
- **Incorrect Yeast Amount:** Using too little yeast can result in insufficient rising. Verify that you're using the correct type and amount of yeast, and ensure it is fresh.

2. Overly Dry Dough:

Dry dough can result from several issues:

- **Insufficient Liquid:** If the dough is too dry, it may not rise properly. Check the recipe for the correct amount of liquid and consider adding a small amount of water to the dough if needed.
- **Flour Type:** Some flours absorb more liquid than others. If you're using a different type of flour, you may need to adjust the liquid content accordingly.

3. Unpleasant Smells:

Unpleasant odors during baking can be a sign of:

- **Expired Ingredients:** Check the expiration dates on your yeast and other ingredients. Old or spoiled ingredients can affect the taste and smell of your bread.
- **Overmixed Dough:** Overmixing can lead to undesirable smells. Follow the recipe's instructions for mixing times to avoid overworking the dough.

4. Uneven Crust:

An uneven crust can be caused by:

- **Uneven Heating:** If your bread machine's heating element is uneven, it can result in an uneven crust. Ensure that the machine is placed on a flat surface and avoid opening the lid during baking.
- **Incorrect Crust Setting:** Make sure to select the correct crust setting for your recipe. Some machines allow you to choose between light, medium, or dark crust options.

By following these tips and troubleshooting common problems, you can confidently start making delicious bread with your bread machine. With practice and attention to detail, you'll soon be able to enjoy the delightful aroma and taste of homemade bread right from your kitchen.

1.4 Essential Ingredients

The foundation of successful bread-making lies in the selection and understanding of the essential ingredients. Each component plays a critical role in the final product, influencing everything from texture and flavor to rise and crust. This section delves into the primary ingredients used in bread-making, including flours, yeasts, and other crucial additives. Understanding these components will help you achieve consistent and delicious results every time you use your bread machine.

Flours: Types and Their Characteristics

Flour is the primary ingredient in bread-making, and its type significantly affects the texture, structure, and flavor of the bread. Different types of flour have varying protein contents, gluten-forming capabilities, and absorbency rates, which influence how the dough behaves during mixing, rising, and baking.

1. Wheat Flour:

Wheat flour is the most common type used in bread-making and comes in several varieties. The primary types of wheat flour include:

- **All-Purpose Flour:** This versatile flour has a moderate protein content, making it suitable for a wide range of bread recipes. It provides a balance between tenderness and structure, which is ideal for beginners. All-purpose flour is milled from a blend of hard and soft wheat, giving it a slightly lower gluten content compared to bread flour. It's a good starting point for experimenting with different recipes.

- **Bread Flour:** With a higher protein content than all-purpose flour, bread flour is specifically designed to provide a strong gluten network, which enhances the structure and chewiness of the bread. The increased protein content helps the dough rise better and hold its shape. Bread flour is particularly useful for recipes that require a more robust structure, such as artisan loaves or sourdough.
- **Whole Wheat Flour:** Whole wheat flour is made from the entire wheat kernel, including the bran, germ, and endosperm. This flour imparts a nutty flavor and dense texture to bread. It absorbs more liquid than white flour and requires longer kneading and rising times. Because it is less refined, whole wheat flour can lead to heavier bread, but it also offers more nutritional benefits. Combining whole wheat flour with all-purpose or bread flour can provide a good balance of flavor and texture.
- **Specialty Flours:** In addition to the common types of wheat flour, there are various specialty flours that can be used to create unique bread. These include:
    - **Rye Flour:** Rye flour contains less gluten than wheat flour, resulting in denser and more flavorful bread. It is often used in combination with wheat flour to create traditional rye bread. Rye flour adds a distinctive earthy taste and contributes to the bread's darker color.
    - **Spelt Flour:** Spelt is an ancient grain that has a nutty, slightly sweet flavor. It has a lower gluten content than wheat flour, so it requires careful handling to achieve the right texture. Spelt flour can be used on its own or blended with other flours.
    - **Oat Flour:** Made from ground oats, oat flour adds a mild, slightly sweet flavor and can be used in combination with other flours. It is often used in gluten-free recipes or as a supplement to increase the nutritional value of bread.

1.5. Gluten-Free Flours

For those with gluten sensitivities or following a gluten-free diet, there are several gluten-free flours available. Each type of gluten-free flour has unique properties and may require adjustments to the recipe:

- **Rice Flour:** Rice flour is commonly used in gluten-free baking. It provides a neutral flavor and is often used in combination with other gluten-free flours to create a balanced texture.
- **Almond Flour:** Made from finely ground almonds, almond flour adds a rich, nutty flavor and moist texture to bread. It is high in protein and healthy fats, making it a popular choice for low-carb and keto recipes.

- **Tapioca Flour:** Tapioca flour, derived from cassava root, is used to add chewiness and elasticity to gluten-free bread. It is often used in conjunction with other gluten-free flours to improve the dough's texture.
- **Chickpea Flour:** Made from ground chickpeas, this flour adds a slightly nutty flavor and is high in protein. It is commonly used in gluten-free baking and can be combined with other flours to enhance the bread's structure.

Yeasts and Their Roles in Baking

Yeast is a living organism that plays a crucial role in bread-making by fermenting the dough. This fermentation process produces carbon dioxide gas, which causes the dough to rise and develop its texture. There are several types of yeast used in baking, each with specific characteristics and applications:

1. Active Dry Yeast:

Active dry yeast is one of the most commonly used types of yeast. It is sold in granulated form and needs to be dissolved in warm water before being added to the dough. This type of yeast requires proofing to ensure that it is active and capable of leavening the dough. To proof active dry yeast, dissolve it in warm water (around 110°F or 43°C) with a small amount of sugar and wait for bubbles or froth to form. This indicates that the yeast is active and ready to use.

2. Instant Yeast:

Instant yeast, also known as rapid-rise or bread machine yeast, is a more convenient option as it can be mixed directly with dry ingredients without needing to be proofed. It has finer granules and works quickly to leaven the dough. Instant yeast is ideal for bread machines, as it allows for faster rising times and more consistent results.

3. Fresh Yeast:

Fresh yeast, also known as cake yeast, comes in a soft, moist block form and must be refrigerated. It has a shorter shelf life compared to dry yeast and needs to be crumbled and dissolved in liquid before use. Fresh yeast is less commonly used but can provide a more complex flavor and is preferred by some bakers for traditional recipes.

4. Yeast Alternatives:

In addition to traditional yeast, there are several alternatives that can be used for leavening:

- **Sourdough Starter:** A sourdough starter is a natural leavening agent made from a mixture of flour and water that ferments over time. It contains wild yeast and bacteria that help the dough rise and develop a tangy flavor. Sourdough bread requires a longer fermentation period and careful handling of the starter.
- **Baking Powder and Baking Soda:** While not true yeasts, baking powder and baking soda can be used as leavening agents in recipes that don't require the dough to rise over an extended period. These chemical leaveners work by releasing carbon dioxide when mixed with liquids and heated.

Other Ingredients: Sugars, Salts, Fats, and Additives

In addition to flour and yeast, several other ingredients are essential for creating well-balanced and flavorful bread. These include sugars, salts, fats, and various additives:

1. Sugars:

Sugars serve multiple purposes in bread-making. They provide food for the yeast, which helps the dough rise, and contribute to the bread's flavor and color. The most common sugars used in bread recipes are:

- **Granulated Sugar:** The standard sugar used in most bread recipes, granulated sugar adds sweetness and helps with yeast fermentation. It is easily incorporated into the dough and dissolves well.
- **Brown Sugar:** Brown sugar contains molasses, which adds a richer flavor and darker color to the bread. It can be used in recipes where a deeper, more caramelized taste is desired.
- **Honey and Molasses:** These natural sweeteners offer unique flavors and additional nutrients. Honey adds moisture and a subtle sweetness, while molasses provides a robust, slightly bitter taste.

2. Salts:

Salt is a crucial ingredient in bread-making for several reasons:

- **Flavor Enhancement:** Salt enhances the overall flavor of the bread, balancing the sweetness and other flavors.

- **Yeast Regulation:** Salt helps to regulate yeast activity, preventing over-fermentation and ensuring a consistent rise.
- **Gluten Development:** Salt strengthens gluten, improving the dough's structure and elasticity.

3. Fats:

Fats contribute to the bread's texture, flavor, and shelf life. Common fats used in bread-making include:

- **Butter:** Adds richness and a tender crumb to the bread. It also improves the bread's shelf life and flavor.
- **Oil:** Vegetable oil, olive oil, or other types of oil can be used to add moisture and create a softer texture. Oil can also help the bread stay fresh for a longer period.
- **Eggs:** Eggs add richness and contribute to the bread's structure and color. They can also help with browning and improve the overall texture.

4. Additives:

Additives such as seeds, nuts, dried fruits, and herbs can enhance the flavor and texture of bread. These ingredients can be added to the dough or used as toppings:

- **Seeds and Nuts:** Add crunch and nutritional value. Common choices include sunflower seeds, sesame seeds, and walnuts.
- **Dried Fruits:** Raisins, cranberries, and apricots add sweetness and texture to bread. They can be mixed into the dough or used as a topping.
- **Herbs and Spices:** Fresh or dried herbs and spices can provide unique flavors and aromas. Examples include rosemary, thyme, and cinnamon.

Understanding these essential ingredients and their roles in bread-making will help you achieve consistent and delicious results with your bread machine. By selecting high-quality ingredients and using them correctly, you'll be able to create a wide variety of breads that are both flavorful and satisfying.

1.6 Baking Techniques

Baking bread is both an art and a science. Mastering the essential techniques of mixing, kneading, proofing, and baking will help you achieve the perfect loaf every time. This section provides a detailed look into the core techniques of bread-making, including mixing and kneading, fermentation and proofing, and baking. Each technique plays a crucial role in determining the texture, flavor, and overall quality of your bread.

Mixing and Kneading: Methods and Timing

The process of mixing and kneading dough is fundamental to bread-making. These steps are crucial for developing gluten, the protein network that gives bread its structure and texture. Proper mixing and kneading ensure that the ingredients are evenly distributed and that the dough achieves the right consistency for optimal rising and baking.

1. Mixing Dough:

The first step in bread-making is mixing the dough. This involves combining all the ingredients—flour, water, yeast, salt, and any additional ingredients such as sugar, fats, or flavorings. Mixing can be done by hand or with a stand mixer fitted with a dough hook.

- **By Hand:** When mixing by hand, use a large bowl and a sturdy spoon or spatula to combine the ingredients. Start by stirring the flour and other dry ingredients together, then gradually add the liquid ingredients. Use your hands to incorporate the ingredients into a cohesive dough. This method allows you to feel the dough's texture and make adjustments as needed.
- **By Stand Mixer:** Using a stand mixer can streamline the mixing process. Combine the dry ingredients in the mixer bowl and then add the wet ingredients. Mix on a low speed until the dough begins to come together. Increase the speed slightly and mix until the dough is smooth and elastic. The dough should pull away from the sides of the bowl and form a ball around the dough hook.

2. Kneading Dough:

Kneading is the process of working the dough to develop gluten. This step is crucial for creating a strong, elastic dough that can hold the gas produced by yeast fermentation. Kneading also helps to distribute the ingredients evenly and improve the dough's texture.

- **By Hand:** Turn the dough out onto a lightly floured surface. Flatten it with your hands and then fold it over itself. Push the dough away from you with the heels of your hands, then fold it back over. Turn the dough a quarter turn and repeat. Knead the dough for about 8-10 minutes, or until it is smooth and elastic. The dough should be slightly tacky but not overly sticky.
- **By Stand Mixer:** If using a stand mixer, continue mixing the dough on a low speed until it becomes smooth and elastic. This usually takes about 5-7 minutes. The dough should be slightly sticky but should pull away from the sides of the bowl. If the dough is too sticky, you can add a small amount of flour; if it is too dry, add a little water.

Proper kneading develops the gluten network, which gives the bread its structure. To test if the dough is kneaded enough, perform the "windowpane test": stretch a small piece of dough between your fingers. If it stretches thin enough to let light through without tearing, the gluten is well-developed.

Proofing: How It Affects Bread Texture

Proofing, or fermentation, is the process where yeast ferments the dough, producing carbon dioxide gas that causes it to rise. Proper proofing is essential for achieving the desired texture and flavor in your bread. The timing and conditions for proofing can greatly affect the outcome of your bread.

1. First Proof:

After kneading, the dough needs to rise for the first time. This is typically done in a warm, draft-free environment. The dough should be placed in a lightly oiled bowl, covered with a damp cloth or plastic wrap, and allowed to rise until it has doubled in size. This process usually takes 1-2 hours, depending on the recipe and the ambient temperature. During this time, the yeast ferments the dough, producing gas bubbles that make it expand.

- **Temperature:** The ideal temperature for proofing is between 75°F and 80°F (24°C to 27°C). If your kitchen is cooler, the rising time may be longer. Conversely, if it is warmer, the dough may rise more quickly. Some bakers use a proofing box or an oven with a light on to maintain a consistent temperature.

- **Humidity:** Maintaining a humid environment can prevent the dough from drying out. Covering the bowl with a damp cloth or plastic wrap helps retain moisture and keeps the surface of the dough from forming a crust.

2. Second Proof:

After the dough has risen, it is usually punched down to release excess gas and then shaped into its final form. The shaped dough undergoes a second proofing, known as the final rise, before baking. This step allows the dough to relax and expand further.

- **Shaping:** Shape the dough according to the recipe, whether it's a loaf, rolls, or another form. Place the shaped dough on a baking sheet or in a loaf pan. Cover it loosely with plastic wrap or a damp cloth and allow it to rise until it has nearly doubled in size. The second proof usually takes about 30-60 minutes.
- **Final Proofing Environment:** Similar to the first proof, the final proof should be done in a warm, draft-free environment. Ensure that the dough is covered to prevent it from drying out.

Proper proofing is crucial for achieving a light, airy texture in the bread. Under-proofed dough may result in dense bread, while over-proofed dough can lead to collapse during baking.

Baking: Ideal Temperatures and Times

Baking is the final step in bread-making, where the dough transforms into a finished loaf. Proper baking temperatures and times are essential for achieving the desired crust, color, and texture. Each bread recipe may have specific baking instructions, but there are general guidelines that apply to most types of bread.

1. Oven Temperature:

The baking temperature for bread typically ranges from 350°F to 475°F (175°C to 245°C), depending on the recipe. Higher temperatures are often used for crusty artisan loaves, while lower temperatures are suitable for softer breads like sandwich loaves.

- **Preheating:** Always preheat the oven before placing the dough inside. This ensures that the bread starts baking at the correct temperature, which helps with oven spring (the initial rise of the bread as it hits the hot oven) and contributes to a well-developed crust.

- **Convection Ovens:** If using a convection oven, which circulates hot air around the food, reduce the baking temperature by 25°F (15°C) from what is specified in the recipe. Convection ovens can produce more even baking and a crispier crust.

2. Baking Times:

Baking times vary depending on the type of bread and the size of the loaf. Smaller loaves and rolls generally bake faster than larger loaves. Most bread recipes provide specific baking times, but here are some general guidelines:

- **Small Loaves and Rolls:** Typically bake for 20-30 minutes.
- **Standard Loaves:** Usually require 30-45 minutes.
- **Artisan and Large Loaves:** Can take 45-60 minutes or longer.

To test if the bread is done, tap the bottom of the loaf; it should sound hollow if fully baked. Alternatively, use an instant-read thermometer to check the internal temperature. Most bread should reach an internal temperature of 190°F to 210°F (88°C to 99°C).

3. Cooling:

Once baked, remove the bread from the oven and let it cool on a wire rack. Cooling the bread allows the steam to escape and prevents the crust from becoming soggy. For best results, avoid cutting into the bread until it has cooled completely, as this allows the crumb to set and makes slicing easier.

In summary, mastering the techniques of mixing, kneading, proofing, and baking is essential for producing high-quality bread. Each step in the process affects the final result, so attention to detail and practice are key. By understanding these fundamental techniques and applying them effectively, you can create a wide range of delicious breads with your bread machine.

1.7 How to Substitute Ingredients

Baking bread with a bread machine can be both rewarding and challenging, especially when it comes to making ingredient substitutions. Whether you are accommodating dietary restrictions, experimenting with new flavors, or trying to create healthier versions of traditional recipes, understanding how to substitute ingredients effectively is crucial. This chapter will explore various alternatives for flour, sugars, and fats, and provide guidance on making adjustments to suit specific dietary needs.

Alternatives for Gluten-Free and Keto Flours

One of the most common reasons for substituting ingredients in bread recipes is to accommodate gluten intolerance or specific dietary preferences such as keto. Traditional wheat flour contains gluten, which is essential for the bread's texture and structure. However, there are several alternative flours that can be used in place of wheat flour to achieve similar results.

1. Gluten-Free Flours:

Gluten-free baking requires a different approach compared to baking with wheat flour. Gluten-free flours lack gluten, so they don't provide the same structure or elasticity as wheat flour. Here are some popular gluten-free flours and their characteristics:

- **Almond Flour:** Made from finely ground almonds, almond flour adds a rich, nutty flavor and moist texture to bread. It's often used in combination with other gluten-free flours to improve the texture and provide structure.
- **Rice Flour:** Rice flour is a staple in gluten-free baking and provides a neutral flavor. It is often used as a base for gluten-free flour blends but can result in a somewhat gritty texture if used alone.
- **Sorghum Flour:** Sorghum flour is high in protein and fiber, making it a good choice for adding nutritional value to gluten-free bread. It has a mild, slightly sweet flavor that complements a variety of other flours.
- **Tapioca Flour:** Tapioca flour, or tapioca starch, is derived from the cassava root and is used primarily as a thickener. It helps to create a chewy texture in gluten-free bread and is often combined with other flours.
- **Oat Flour:** Oat flour can be used in gluten-free baking if certified gluten-free oats are used. It adds a mild, slightly sweet flavor and can improve the texture of gluten-free bread.

When substituting gluten-free flours, it's important to use a blend of flours to achieve the right texture and structure. Many commercial gluten-free flour blends are formulated to mimic the properties of wheat flour and include additional ingredients such as xanthan gum or guar gum to provide elasticity and binding.

2. Keto Flours:

For those following a ketogenic (keto) diet, which is low in carbohydrates and high in fats, traditional flours are replaced with low-carb alternatives. Keto-friendly flours include:

- **Almond Flour:** Almond flour is a popular choice for keto baking due to its low carbohydrate content and high fat content. It provides a moist texture and a mild nutty flavor.
- **Coconut Flour:** Coconut flour is another low-carb option that adds a subtle coconut flavor to baked goods. It is highly absorbent, so recipes often require more liquid than those made with other flours.

- **Flaxseed Meal:** Ground flaxseeds provide a source of fiber and omega-3 fatty acids. It can be used to add texture and nutritional benefits to keto bread recipes.

When baking with keto flours, it is often necessary to experiment with different ratios and combinations to achieve the desired results. These flours do not behave the same way as wheat flour, so recipes may require adjustments in liquid content and other ingredients.

Substitutions for Sugars and Fats

In addition to flour substitutions, altering sugars and fats is another common practice to adapt recipes for dietary preferences or health considerations. Each ingredient plays a distinct role in bread-making, so understanding their functions will help you make effective substitutions.

1. Sugar Substitutes:

Sugar serves multiple purposes in bread-making, including adding sweetness, contributing to browning, and aiding in yeast fermentation. When replacing sugar, consider the following alternatives:

- **Honey:** Honey is a natural sweetener that can be used as a one-to-one substitute for sugar. It adds moisture and a distinct flavor to bread. However, because honey is liquid, you may need to reduce other liquid ingredients in the recipe.
- **Maple Syrup:** Maple syrup is another liquid sweetener that can replace sugar in bread recipes. It imparts a unique flavor and adds moisture, similar to honey. Adjust the liquid content accordingly.
- **Stevia:** Stevia is a non-caloric sweetener derived from the leaves of the stevia plant. It is much sweeter than sugar, so use it in smaller amounts. It doesn't provide the same browning effect as sugar, so you may need to adjust baking times and temperatures.
- **Erythritol:** Erythritol is a sugar alcohol that provides sweetness without the calories and carbs of sugar. It can be used in a one-to-one ratio with sugar, but it may not provide the same browning or texture.

2. Fat Substitutes:

Fats contribute to the flavor, texture, and moisture of bread. When substituting fats, consider the following options:

- **Unsweetened Applesauce:** Applesauce can replace some or all of the fat in a recipe, adding moisture and a slight sweetness. It works well in quick breads and muffins but may not provide the same richness as butter or oil.
- **Greek Yogurt:** Greek yogurt can be used to replace some of the fat in bread recipes. It adds moisture and a tangy flavor while providing additional protein. Adjust the recipe to account for the added liquid.

- **Avocado:** Mashed avocado can be used as a substitute for butter or oil, providing healthy fats and a creamy texture. It may slightly alter the flavor of the bread.
- **Butter or Margarine:** When replacing butter or margarine, choose a substitute with a similar fat content and texture. For example, if using a margarine blend or a plant-based butter, ensure that it is suitable for baking.

Adjusting recipes to accommodate different sugars and fats requires careful consideration of how these substitutes will affect the final product. Experimenting with small batches and making incremental changes can help you find the best substitutions for your needs.

Adjustments for Specific Dietary Needs

In addition to gluten-free and keto diets, there are many other dietary needs that may require ingredient substitutions. Whether you are baking for someone with a food allergy, a specific health condition, or a personal preference, understanding how to make these adjustments will help you create delicious and suitable bread.

1. Dairy-Free Options:

For those who are lactose intolerant or following a dairy-free diet, there are several alternatives to dairy ingredients:

- **Non-Dairy Milks:** Almond milk, soy milk, and oat milk can be used as substitutes for cow's milk in bread recipes. Choose an unsweetened variety to avoid altering the recipe's sweetness.
- **Dairy-Free Butters:** Plant-based butters or oils can replace dairy butter. Ensure that the substitute has a similar fat content to achieve the right texture.

2. Egg Substitutes:

Eggs are often used in bread recipes for their binding properties and to add moisture. For those avoiding eggs, consider these alternatives:

- **Flaxseed Meal:** Combine one tablespoon of flaxseed meal with three tablespoons of water to create a "flax egg." This mixture can replace one egg in most recipes.
- **Chia Seeds:** Similar to flaxseeds, chia seeds can be mixed with water to create a gel-like substance that works as an egg substitute.
- **Applesauce:** Unsweetened applesauce can replace eggs in recipes, providing moisture and a slight sweetness.

3. Low-Sodium Options:

For those reducing sodium intake, consider the following substitutions:

- **Reduced-Sodium Salt:** Use a reduced-sodium salt or simply cut back on the amount of salt in the recipe.
- **Herbs and Spices:** Enhance flavor with herbs and spices instead of salt. Garlic powder, onion powder, and various dried herbs can add complexity without extra sodium.

By understanding how to substitute ingredients effectively, you can adapt your bread recipes to meet dietary restrictions, personal preferences, and health goals. Each substitution may require some experimentation to achieve the desired results, so don't hesitate to make small adjustments and test different combinations. With practice and patience, you can create delicious bread that fits your unique needs and preferences.

Chapter 2: Classic Bread Recipes

2.1 Traditional White Bread

Preparation Time:	Cooking Time:	Total Time:
10 minutes	3 hours	3 hours 10 minutes

Nutritional Information (per slice):

Calories: 160	**Carbohydrates:** 28 g	**Sodium:** 300 mg
Protein: 4 g	**Fat:** 2 g	**Sugars:** 3 g

Bread Machine Setting: Basic (1.5 lb loaf)   **Quantity:** 1.5 lb loaf

Ingredients:

- 1 cup (240 ml) warm water
- 2 tbsp (28 g) unsalted butter, softened
- 2 tbsp (25 g) sugar
- 3 cups (360 g) bread flour
- 1 1/2 tsp (8 g) salt
- 2 1/4 tsp (7 g) active dry yeast

Instructions:

1. **Load Ingredients:** Add water, butter, sugar, flour, salt, and yeast to the bread machine pan in the order recommended by the manufacturer.
2. **Select Settings:** Choose the **Basic** bread setting with a **Medium** or **Dark** crust setting, depending on your preference.
3. **Start and Monitor:** Press Start and allow the machine to complete the full cycle.
4. **Cool:** Once baking is complete, remove the bread from the pan and let it cool on a wire rack before slicing.

Expert Tips:

- **Crispy Crust:** For a crisper crust, select the **Dark** crust setting.
- **Soft Texture:** Ensure the butter is fully softened to help create a tender crumb.

2.2 Whole Wheat Bread

Preparation Time:	Cooking Time:	Total Time:
10 minutes	3 hours 30 minutes	3 hours 40 minutes

Nutritional Information (per slice):

Calories: 170	**Carbohydrates:** 30 g	**Sodium:** 310 mg
Protein: 5 g	**Fat:** 3 g	**Sugars:** 4

B. Machine Setting: Whole Wheat 1.5 lb loaf   **Quantity:** 1.5 lb loaf

Ingredients:

- 1 1/4 cups (300 ml) warm water
- 2 tbsp (28 g) unsalted butter, softened
- 2 tbsp (25 g) honey or sugar
- 3 cups (360 g) whole wheat flour
- 1 1/2 tsp (8 g) salt
- 2 tbsp (20 g) powdered milk
- 2 1/4 tsp (7 g) active dry yeast

Instructions:

1. **Load Ingredients:** Add water, butter, honey, flour, salt, powdered milk, and yeast to the bread machine pan in the order recommended by the manufacturer.
2. **Select Settings:** Choose the **Whole Wheat** bread setting for a soft and moist whole wheat loaf.
3. **Monitor Consistency:** Check the dough consistency during kneading. If too dry, add a tablespoon of water.
4. **Cool:** Once baking is complete, remove the bread and let it cool on a wire rack before slicing.

Expert Tips:

- **Moisture:** Whole wheat flour absorbs more water, so monitor dough consistency and adjust as needed.
- **Honey Addition:** Honey adds natural sweetness and helps keep the bread moist.

2.3 Seed and Nut Bread

Preparation Time:	Cooking Time:	Total Time:
10 minutes	3 hours 20 minutes	3 hours 30 minutes

Nutritional Information (per slice):

Calories: 190	Carbohydrates: 28 g	Sodium: 300 mg
Protein: 6 g	Fat: 6 g	Sugars: 2 g

Bread Machine Setting: Basic (1.5 lb loaf) **Quantity:** 1.5 lb loaf

Ingredients:

- 1 cup (240 ml) warm water
- 2 tbsp (28 g) unsalted butter, softened
- 2 tbsp (25 g) sugar
- 2 1/2 cups (300 g) bread flour
- 1/2 cup (60 g) whole wheat flour
- 1/2 cup (60 g) mixed seeds (e.g., sunflower, sesame, flax)
- 1/2 cup (60 g) chopped nuts (e.g., walnuts, almonds)
- 1 1/2 tsp (8 g) salt
- 2 1/4 tsp (7 g) active dry yeast

Instructions:

1. **Load Ingredients:** Add water, butter, sugar, flours, salt, and yeast to the bread machine pan.
2. **Add Nuts and Seeds:** When the machine beeps (around the kneading stage), add the seeds and nuts.
3. **Select Settings:** Choose the **Basic** bread setting.
4. **Cool:** Remove the bread from the pan after baking and cool on a wire rack before slicing.

Expert Tips:

- **Nuts and Seeds:** Add nuts and seeds later in the kneading process to avoid them breaking down too much.
- **Freshness:** Store this bread in an airtight container to keep it fresh longer.

2.4 Milk and Butter Bread

Preparation Time:	Cooking Time:	Total Time:
10 minutes	3 hours	3 hours 10 minutes

Nutritional Information (per slice):

Calories: 180	**Carbohydrates:** 28 g	**Sodium:** 320 mg
Protein: 5 g	**Fat:** 5 g	**Sugars:** 4

Bread Machine Setting: Sweet (1.5 lb loaf)   **Quantity:** 1.5 lb loaf

Ingredients:

- 1 cup (240 ml) warm milk
- 1/4 cup (60 g) unsalted butter, melted
- 2 tbsp (25 g) sugar

- 3 cups (360 g) bread flour
- 1 1/2 tsp (8 g) salt
- 2 1/4 tsp (7 g) active dry yeast

Instructions:

1. **Load Ingredients:** Add warm milk, melted butter, sugar, flour, salt, and yeast to the bread machine pan.
2. **Select Settings:** Choose the **Sweet** bread setting.
3. **Monitor:** Allow the machine to complete the full cycle.
4. **Cool:** After baking, remove the bread from the pan and let it cool on a wire rack before serving.

Expert Tips:

- **Soft Crust:** For a softer crust, brush the loaf with melted butter immediately after baking.
- **Rich Flavor:** Use whole milk for a richer flavor and texture.

2.5 Rustic Bread

Preparation Time:	**Cooking Time:**	**Total Time:**
10 minutes	3 hours 20 minutes	3 hours 30 minutes

Nutritional Information (per slice):

Calories: 150	**Carbohydrates:** 26 g	**Sodium:** 300 mg
Protein: 4 g	**Fat:** 2 g	**Sugars:** 1 g

Bread Machine Setting: French (1.5 lb loaf)   **Quantity:** 1.5 lb loaf

Ingredients:

- 1 1/4 cups (300 ml) warm water
- 2 tbsp (28 g) unsalted butter, softened
- 3 cups (360 g) bread flour
- 1/2 cup (60 g) whole wheat flour

- 1 tsp (5 g) salt
- 1 tsp (5 g) sugar
- 2 1/4 tsp (7 g) active dry yeast

Instructions:

1. **Load Ingredients:** Add warm water, butter, flours, salt, sugar, and yeast to the bread machine pan.
2. **Select Settings:** Choose the **French** bread setting to achieve a thicker crust and chewy interior.
3. **Cool:** Once the bread is baked, remove it from the pan and cool on a wire rack before slicing.

Expert Tips:

- **Crust Thickness:** The French setting creates a thicker crust, perfect for rustic bread.
- **Flour Variety:** Experiment with different flours like rye or spelt for a more complex flavor.

2.6 Corn Bread

Preparation Time:
10 minutes

Cooking Time:
3 hours

Total Time:
3 hours 10 minutes

Nutritional Information (per slice):

Calories: 160	**Carbohydrates:** 30 g	**Sodium:** 320 mg
Protein: 4 g	**Fat:** 2 g	**Sugars:** 2 g

Bread Machine Setting: Basic (1.5 lb loaf)   **Quantity:** 1.5 lb loaf

Ingredients:

- 1 cup (240 ml) warm water
- 1/4 cup (60 ml) vegetable oil
- 1 cup (120 g) cornmeal
- 2 cups (240 g) bread flour

- 1 tbsp (15 g) sugar
- 1 tsp (5 g) salt
- 2 1/4 tsp (7 g) active dry yeast

Instructions:

1. **Load Ingredients:** Add water, oil, cornmeal, flour, sugar, salt, and yeast to the bread machine pan.
2. **Select Settings:** Choose the **Basic** bread setting to ensure even cooking and a slight crunch from the cornmeal.

3. **Monitor:** Allow the machine to complete the baking cycle.
4. **Cool:** After baking, remove the bread from the pan and let it cool on a wire rack before slicing.

Expert Tips:

- **Texture:** The cornmeal adds a slightly gritty texture, perfect for those who enjoy a bit of crunch.
- **Sweetness:** Add an extra tablespoon of sugar for a sweeter corn bread

Chapter 3: International Breads

3.1 Italian Bread (Ciabatta)

Preparation Time:	**Cooking Time:**	**Total Time:**
10 minutes	2 hours	2 hours 10 minutes

Nutritional Information (per 1 oz serving):

Calories: 130	**Carbohydrates:** 25 g	**Sodium:** 220 mg
Protein: 4 g	**Fat:** 1 g	**Sugars:** 1 g

Bread Machine Setting: Dough   **Quantity:** 1 ciabatta loaf

Ingredients:

- 1 1/2 cups (360 ml) warm water
- 2 tbsp (30 ml) olive oil
- 3 1/2 cups (420 g) all-purpose flour
- 1/2 cup (60 g) bread flour
- 2 1/4 tsp (7 g) active dry yeast
- 1 tsp (5 g) salt

Instructions:

1. **Combine Ingredients:** Add warm water, olive oil, flour, and salt to the bread machine pan. Sprinkle yeast on top.
2. **Mix and Knead:** Select the **Dough** setting and press Start.
3. **First Rise:** Allow the dough to rise in the bread machine until doubled in size.
4. **Shape and Bake:** Transfer the dough to a floured surface, shape it into a rectangle, and let it rise again. Preheat the oven to 425°F (220°C) and bake on a floured baking sheet for 20-25 minutes until the crust is golden brown.

Expert Tips:

- **Crispy Crust:** For an extra crispy crust, spray water into the oven during the first 10 minutes of baking.
- **Perfect Shape:** Use a baking stone for a more authentic ciabatta shape.

3.1 Italian Bread (Focaccia)

Preparation Time: 15 minutes

Cooking Time: 2 hours (including rising and baking)

Total Time: 2 hours 15 minutes

Nutritional Information (per 1 oz serving):

Calories: 140	**Carbohydrates:** 25 g	**Sodium:** 250 mg
Protein: 4 g	**Fat:** 3 g	**Sugars:** 1 g

Bread Machine Setting: Dough   **Quantity:** 1 focaccia

Ingredients:

- 1 1/2 cups (360 ml) warm water
- 1/4 cup (60 ml) olive oil
- 3 1/2 cups (420 g) all-purpose flour
- 1/2 cup (60 g) bread flour

2 1/4 tsp (7 g) active dry yeast

1 tsp (5 g) salt

Fresh rosemary and sea salt for topping

Instructions:

1. **Combine Ingredients:** Add warm water, olive oil, flour, and salt to the bread machine pan. Sprinkle yeast on top.
2. **Mix and Knead:** Select the **Dough** setting and press Start.
3. **First Rise:** Allow the dough to rise in the bread machine until doubled in size.
4. **Shape and Bake:** Transfer the dough to a greased baking sheet, dimple with your fingers, and top with rosemary and sea salt. Bake at 400°F (200°C) for 20-25 minutes until golden.

Expert Tips:

- **Dimpling:** Pressing your fingers into the dough before baking helps create those signature focaccia pockets.
- **Olive Oil:** Drizzle extra olive oil over the dough before baking for a richer flavor.

3.2 French Bread (Baguette)

Preparation Time:
10 minutes

Cooking Time:
2 hours

Total Time:
2 hours 10 minutes

Nutritional Information (per 1 oz serving):

Calories: 120

Carbohydrates: 23 g

Sodium: 220 mg

Protein: 4 g

Fat: 1 g

Sugars: 1 g

Bread Machine Setting: Dough

Quantity: 2 baguettes

Ingredients:

- 1 1/2 cups (360 ml) warm water
- 3 1/2 cups (420 g) bread flour
- 2 1/4 tsp (7 g) active dry yeast
- 1 tsp (5 g) salt

Instructions:

1. **Combine Ingredients:** Add warm water, flour, and salt to the bread machine pan. Sprinkle yeast on top.
2. **Mix and Knead:** Select the **Dough** setting and press Start.
3. **First Rise:** Let the dough rise in the bread machine until doubled in size.
4. **Shape and Bake:** Shape the dough into baguettes, place on a floured baking sheet, and let rise again. Preheat the oven to 450°F (230°C). Bake for 20-25 minutes, spraying the oven with water for a crispy crust.

Expert Tips:

- **Steam:** Use a baking tray with water in the oven to create steam for a crispy crust.
- **Scoring:** Score the top of the baguette with a sharp knife before baking for a professional look:

3.2 French Bread (Pain de Campagne)

Preparation Time:
15 minutes

Cooking Time:
2 hours 30 minutes

Total Time:
2 hours 45 minutes

Nutritional Information (per 1 oz serving):

Calories: 130   Carbohydrates: 24 g   Sodium: 240 mg
Protein: 4 g   Fat: 1 g   Sugars: 1 g

Bread Machine Setting: Dough   **Quantity:** 1 loaf

Ingredients:

- 1 1/2 cups (360 ml) warm water
- 1 cup (120 g) whole wheat flour
- 2 1/2 cups (300 g) bread flour
- 2 1/4 tsp (7 g) active dry yeast
- 1 tsp (5 g) salt

Instructions:

1. **Combine Ingredients:** Add warm water, flours, and salt to the bread machine pan. Sprinkle yeast on top.
2. **Mix and Knead:** Select the **Dough** setting and press Start.
3. **First Rise:** Let the dough rise in the bread machine until doubled in size.
4. **Shape and Bake:** Transfer dough to a floured Dutch oven or a baking stone. Let rise again and bake at 450°F (230°C) for 30-35 minutes.

Expert Tips:

- **Dutch Oven:** Baking in a Dutch oven traps steam and gives the bread a perfect crust.
- **Rustic Shape:** Shape the loaf loosely for an authentic, rustic appearance.

3.3 Asian Bread (Mantou - Chinese Steamed Buns)

Preparation Time: **Cooking Time:**   **Total Time:**
15 minutes   45 minutes   1 ho

Nutritional Information (per 1 oz serving):

Calories: 110   Carbohydrates: 20 g   Sodium: 120 mg
Protein: 3 g   Fat: 1 g   Sugars: 1 g

Bread Machine Setting: Dough   **Quantity:** 12 buns

Ingredients:

- 1 cup (240 ml) warm water
- 2 tbsp (30 g) sugar
- 3 cups (360 g) all-purpose flour
- 2 1/4 tsp (7 g) active dry yeast
- 1/2 tsp (2 g) salt

Instructions:

1. **Combine Ingredients:** Add warm water, sugar, flour, and salt to the bread machine pan. Sprinkle yeast on top.
2. **Mix and Knead:** Select the **Dough** setting and press Start.
3. **First Rise:** Let the dough rise in the bread machine until doubled in size.
4. **Shape and Steam:** Divide the dough into 12 pieces, shape into balls, and let rise for 20 minutes. Steam the buns in a bamboo steamer over boiling water for 15 minutes.

Expert Tips:

- **Soft Texture:** Keep the steamer lid slightly ajar to prevent water droplets from falling on the buns.
- **Smooth Surface:** Knead the dough well before steaming to ensure a smooth bun surface.

3.3 Asian Bread (Ramen Bread)

Preparation Time:	**Cooking Time:**	**Total Time:**
15 minutes	1 hour 30 minutes	1 hour 45 minutes

Nutritional Information (per 1 oz serving):

Calories: 120	**Carbohydrates:** 23 g	**Sodium:** 200 mg
Protein: 4 g	**Fat:** 2 g	**Sugars:** 1 g

Bread Machine Setting: Dough   **Quantity:** 1 loaf

Ingredients:

- 1 cup (240 ml) warm water
- 3 1/2 cups (420 g) bread flour
- 1/4 cup (60 ml) soy sauce
- 2 tbsp (30 g) sugar
- 2 1/4 tsp (7 g) active dry yeast
- 1 tsp (5 g) salt

Instructions:

1. **Combine Ingredients:** Add warm water, soy sauce, sugar, flour, and salt to the bread machine pan. Sprinkle yeast on top.
2. **Mix and Knead:** Select the **Dough** setting and press Start.

3. **First Rise:** Let the dough rise in the bread machine until doubled in size.
4. **Shape and Bake:** Transfer the dough to a loaf pan, let rise again, and bake at 375°F (190°C) for 30-35 minutes.

Expert Tips:

- **Soy Flavor:** Soy sauce adds a unique umami flavor to the bread.
- **Soft Crust:** Brush the crust with melted butter after baking for a softer texture.

Chapter 4: Whole wheat Bread

4.1 Classic Whole Wheat Bread

Preparation Time:
10 minutes

Cooking Time:
3 hours

Total Time:
3 hours 10 minutes

Nutritional Information (per 1 oz serving):

Calories: 120

Carbohydrates: 22 g

Sodium: 180 mg

Protein: 5 g

Fat: 2 g

Sugars: 3 g

Bread Machine Setting: Whole Wheat

Quantity: 1 loaf

Ingredients:

- 1 1/2 cups (360 ml) warm water
- 1/4 cup (60 g) vegetable oil
- 1/4 cup (60 g) honey
- 1 1/2 tsp (9 g) salt
- 2 cups (240 g) whole wheat flour

- 1 cup (120 g) all-purpose flour
- 2 1/4 tsp (7 g) active dry yeast
- 2 tbsp (16 g) vital wheat gluten (optional, for a softer texture)

Instructions:

1. **Add Ingredients:** Pour warm water, vegetable oil, and honey into the bread machine pan. Add salt.
2. **Add Flours and Yeast:** Add whole wheat flour, all-purpose flour, and yeast. If using, add vital wheat gluten. Select the **Whole Wheat** setting and press Start.
3. **Monitor Dough:** Check the dough consistency during the first kneading cycle. It should be slightly sticky but manageable. Add more flour if necessary.
4. **Bake:** Allow the bread machine to complete the baking cycle. Let the bread cool on a wire rack before slicing.

Expert Tips:

- **Vital Wheat Gluten:** Enhances the texture of whole wheat bread by improving elasticity.
- **Water Temperature:** Use warm water to activate the yeast effectively.

4.2 Whole Wheat Bread with Seeds

Preparation Time:
15 minutes

Cooking Time:
3 hours

Total Time:
3 hours 15 minutes

Nutritional Information (per 1 oz serving):

| Calories: 130 | Carbohydrates: 23 g | Sodium: 200 mg |
| Protein: 6 g | Fat: 4 g | Sugars: 4 g |

Bread Machine Setting: Whole Wheat   **Quantity:** 1 loaf

Ingredients:

- 1 1/2 cups (360 ml) warm water
- 1/4 cup (60 g) vegetable oil
- 1/4 cup (60 g) honey
- 1 1/2 tsp (9 g) salt
- 2 cups (240 g) whole wheat flour

- 1 cup (120 g) all-purpose flour
- 2 1/4 tsp (7 g) active dry yeast
- 2 tbsp (16 g) chia seeds
- 2 tbsp (16 g) flaxseeds

2 tbsp (16 g) sunflower seeds

Instructions:

1. **Add Ingredients:** Pour warm water, vegetable oil, and honey into the bread machine pan. Add salt.

2. **Add Flours and Seeds:** Add whole wheat flour, all-purpose flour, and yeast. Add chia seeds, flaxseeds, and sunflower seeds. Select the **Whole Wheat** setting and press Start.

3. **Monitor Dough:** Check the dough consistency during the first kneading cycle. Seeds should be evenly distributed. Add more flour if necessary.

4. **Bake:** Allow the bread machine to complete the baking cycle. Let the bread cool on a wire rack before slicing.

Expert Tips:

- **Seed Addition:** Adding seeds during the last part of the kneading ensures they are evenly mixed without being crushed.

- **Flaxseed Hydration:** Soaking flaxseeds before adding can improve their integration into the dough.

4.3 Whole Wheat Bread with Nuts and Raisins

| **Preparation Time:** | **Cooking Time:** | **Total Time:** |
| 20 minutes | 3 hours | 3 hours 20 minutes |

Nutritional Information (per 1 oz serving):

| Calories: 140 | Carbohydrates: 24 g | Sodium: 210 mg |
| Protein: 6 g | Fat: 4 g | Sugars: 8 g |

Bread Machine Setting: Whole Wheat   **Quantity:** 1 loaf

Ingredients:

- 1 1/2 cups (360 ml) warm water
- 1/4 cup (60 g) vegetable oil

- 1/4 cup (60 g) honey
- 1 1/2 tsp (9 g) salt

- 2 cups (240 g) whole wheat flour
- 1 cup (120 g) all-purpose flour
- 2 1/4 tsp (7 g) active dry yeast

- 1/2 cup (75 g) chopped walnuts
- 1/2 cup (75 g) raisins

Instructions:

1. **Add Ingredients:** Pour warm water, vegetable oil, and honey into the bread machine pan. Add salt.

2. **Add Flours and Yeast:** Add whole wheat flour, all-purpose flour, and yeast. Add chopped walnuts and raisins. Select the **Whole Wheat** setting and press Start.

3. **Add Nuts and Raisins:** If your machine has an audible signal for add-ins, add nuts and raisins when prompted.

4. **Bake:** Allow the bread machine to complete the baking cycle. Let the bread cool on a wire rack before slicing.

Expert Tips:

- **Fruit Rehydration:** Soak raisins in warm water before adding to prevent them from drying out the bread.

- **Nut Texture:** Chop nuts finely if you prefer a more even distribution throughout the loaf.

4.4 Whole Wheat Bread with Spices

Preparation Time:	Cooking Time:	Total Time:
15 minutes	3 hours	3 hours 15 minutes

Nutritional Information (per 1 oz serving):

Calories: 125	**Carbohydrates:** 22 g	**Sodium:** 190 mg
Protein: 5 g	**Fat:** 3 g	**Sugars:** 4 g

Bread Machine Setting: Whole Wheat   **Quantity:** 1 loaf

Ingredients:

- 1 1/2 cups (360 ml) warm water
- 1/4 cup (60 g) vegetable oil
- 1/4 cup (60 g) honey
- 1 1/2 tsp (9 g) salt
- 2 cups (240 g) whole wheat flour

- 1 cup (120 g) all-purpose flour
- 2 1/4 tsp (7 g) active dry yeast
- 1 tsp (2 g) ground cinnamon
- 1/2 tsp (1 g) ground ginger
- 1/4 tsp (1 g) ground cloves

Instructions:

1. **Add Ingredients:** Pour warm water, vegetable oil, and honey into the bread machine pan. Add salt.

2. **Add Flours and Spices:** Add whole wheat flour, all-purpose flour, yeast, and spices. Select the **Whole Wheat** setting and press Start.

3. **Monitor Dough:** Ensure spices are well-mixed into the dough. Adjust flour if the dough is too sticky.

4. **Bake:** Allow the bread machine to complete the baking cycle. Let the bread cool on a wire rack before slicing.

Expert Tips:

- **Spice Balance:** Adjust spices to taste. More cinnamon can add warmth, while ginger and cloves add depth.

- **Even Distribution:** Mix spices with the flour to ensure an even distribution throughout the dough.

4.5 Whole Wheat Bread with Yogurt

Preparation Time:	Cooking Time:	Total Time:
15 minutes	3 hours	3 hours 15 minutes

Nutritional Information (per 1 oz serving):

Calories: 115	**Carbohydrates:** 22 g	**Sodium:** 180 mg
Protein: 6 g	**Fat:** 2 g	**Sugars:** 4 g

Bread Machine Setting: Whole Wheat   **Quantity:** 1 loaf

Ingredients:

- 1 cup (240 ml) warm milk
- 1/2 cup (120 g) plain yogurt
- 1/4 cup (60 g) vegetable oil
- 1/4 cup (60 g) honey
- 1 1/2 tsp (9 g) salt
- 2 cups (240 g) whole wheat flour
- 1 cup (120 g) all-purpose flour
- 2 1/4 tsp (7 g) active dry yeast

Instructions:

1. **Add Ingredients:** Pour warm milk, yogurt, vegetable oil, and honey into the bread machine pan. Add salt.

2. **Add Flours and Yeast:** Add whole wheat flour, all-purpose flour, and yeast. Select the **Whole Wheat** setting and press Start.

3. **Monitor Dough:** The dough should be slightly sticky. Adjust with a little flour if necessary.

4. **Bake:** Allow the bread machine to complete the baking cycle. Let the bread cool on a wire rack before slicing.

Expert Tips:

- **Yogurt Benefits:** Yogurt adds moisture and can help achieve a lighter texture. Make sure it's plain yogurt without added flavors or sugar.

- **Dough Consistency:** Adjust flour or milk as needed to get the right dough consistency.

4.6 Whole Wheat Bread with Honey

Preparation Time:	**Cooking Time:**	**Total Time:**
15 minutes	3 hours	3 hours 15 minutes

Nutritional Information (per 1 oz serving):

Calories: 130	**Carbohydrates:** 24 g	**Sodium:** 190 mg
Protein: 5 g	**Fat:** 3 g	**Sugars:** 6 g

Bread Machine Setting: Whole Wheat   **Quantity:** 1 loaf

Ingredients:

- 1 1/2 cups (360 ml) warm water
- 1/4 cup (60 g) vegetable oil
- 1/2 cup (120 g) honey
- 1 1/2 tsp (9 g) salt
- 2 cups (240 g) whole wheat flour
- 1 cup (120 g) all-purpose flour
- 2 1/4 tsp (7 g) active dry yeast

Instructions:

1. **Add Ingredients:** Pour warm water, vegetable oil, and honey into the bread machine pan. Add salt.

2. **Add Flours and Yeast:** Add whole wheat flour, all-purpose flour, and yeast. Select the **Whole Wheat** setting and press Start.

3. **Monitor Dough:** Honey adds extra moisture, so adjust flour if the dough is too sticky.

4. **Bake:** Allow the bread machine to complete the baking cycle. Let the bread cool on a wire rack before slicing.

Expert Tips:

- **Honey Application:** For a darker, glossy crust, brush the loaf with a mixture of honey and water before baking.

- **Flavor Balance:** Adjust honey to suit your sweetness preference.

4.7 Whole Wheat Bread with Slow Rise

Preparation Time:
15 minutes

Cooking Time:
4 hours

Total Time:
4 hours 15 minutes

Nutritional Information (per 1 oz serving):

Calories: 125
Protein: 5 g

Carbohydrates: 22 g
Fat: 2 g

Sodium: 190 mg
Sugars: 4 g

Bread Machine Setting: Custom or Slow Rise   **Quantity:** 1 loaf

Ingredients:

- 1 1/2 cups (360 ml) warm water
- 1/4 cup (60 g) vegetable oil
- 1/4 cup (60 g) honey
- 1 1/2 tsp (9 g) salt

- 2 cups (240 g) whole wheat flour
- 1 cup (120 g) all-purpose flour
- 2 1/4 tsp (7 g) active dry yeast

Instructions:

1. **Add Ingredients:** Pour warm water, vegetable oil, and honey into the bread machine pan. Add salt.

2. **Add Flours and Yeast:** Add whole wheat flour, all-purpose flour, and yeast. Select the **Custom** or **Slow Rise** setting if available.

3. **Adjust Rise Time:** If your machine does not have a slow rise setting, allow the dough to rise for an extra hour before baking.

4. **Bake:** Allow the bread machine to complete the baking cycle. Let the bread cool on a wire rack before slicing.

Expert Tips:

- **Slow Rise Benefits:** A slower rise allows for a denser texture and richer flavor. Monitor dough closely during the extra rise time.

- **Machine Settings:** Check your bread machine's manual for custom or extended rise settings.

Chapter 5: Nutritious and Healthy Bread

5.1 Whole Almond Flour Bread

Preparation Time:
10 minutes

Cooking Time:
3 hours

Total Time:
3 hours 10 minutes

Nutritional Information (per 1 oz serving):

Calories: 180

Carbohydrates: 6 g

Sodium: 220 mg

Protein: 7 g

Fat: 16 g

Sugars: 1 g

Bread Machine Setting: Whole Wheat

Quantity: 1 loaf

Ingredients:

- 1 cup (240 ml) warm water
- 1/4 cup (60 ml) olive oil
- 1/4 cup (60 g) honey
- 2 cups (200 g) almond flour
- 1/2 cup (60 g) coconut flour
- 1/2 tsp (2 g) salt
- 1/4 tsp (1 g) baking soda
- 1 tbsp (9 g) xanthan gum
- 3 large eggs

Instructions:

1. **Add Ingredients:** Pour warm water, olive oil, and honey into the bread machine pan. Add salt.
2. **Add Flours and Binding Agents:** Add almond flour, coconut flour, baking soda, and xanthan gum. Gently mix.
3. **Add Eggs:** Crack eggs into the pan and mix with a spatula.
4. **Select Setting:** Choose the **Whole Wheat** setting and press Start. The batter will be thicker than typical bread dough.

5. **Bake:** Allow the bread machine to complete the cycle. Let cool before slicing.

Expert Tips:

- **Xanthan Gum:** Essential for binding as almond flour lacks gluten.
- **Texture Check:** The dough will be thicker; ensure it's evenly mixed.

5.2 Seed and Superfood Bread

Preparation Time:
15 minutes

Cooking Time:
3 hours

Total Time:
3 hours 15 minutes

Nutritional Information (per 1 oz serving):

Calories: 140

Carbohydrates: 22 g

Sodium: 190 mg

Protein: 6 g

Fat: 5 g

Sugars: 3

Bread Machine Setting: Whole Wheat

Quantity: 1 loaf

Ingredients:

- 1 1/2 cups (360 ml) warm water
- 1/4 cup (60 ml) olive oil
- 2 tbsp (30 g) honey
- 2 cups (240 g) whole wheat flour
- 1/2 cup (60 g) quinoa, cooked
- 1/4 cup (30 g) chia seeds
- 1/4 cup (30 g) flaxseeds
- 2 1/4 tsp (7 g) active dry yeast
- 1 1/2 tsp (9 g) salt

Instructions:

1. **Add Ingredients:** Pour warm water, olive oil, and honey into the bread machine pan. Add salt.
2. **Add Flours and Seeds:** Add whole wheat flour, cooked quinoa, chia seeds, flaxseeds, and yeast.
3. **Select Setting:** Choose the **Whole Wheat** setting and press Start.
4. **Monitor Dough:** Check consistency. If needed, add a bit more water if the dough appears dry.
5. **Bake:** Allow the bread machine to complete the cycle. Cool on a wire rack before slicing.

Expert Tips:

- **Quinoa Preparation:** Ensure quinoa is well-cooked and cooled before adding.
- **Even Mixing:** Add seeds during the kneading cycle for even distribution.

5.3 Carrot and Pumpkin Bread

Preparation Time:
20 minutes

Cooking Time:
3 hours

Total Time:
3 hours 20 minutes

Nutritional Information (per 1 oz serving):

Calories: 130
Protein: 4 g

Carbohydrates: 22 g
Fat: 4 g

Sodium: 210 mg
Sugars: 5 g

Bread Machine Setting: Whole Wheat

Quantity: 1 loaf

Ingredients:

- 1 cup (240 ml) warm milk
- 1/2 cup (120 g) pumpkin puree
- 1/2 cup (120 g) grated carrot
- 1/4 cup (60 ml) olive oil
- 2 tbsp (30 g) honey

- 2 cups (240 g) whole wheat flour
- 1/2 cup (60 g) all-purpose flour
- 2 1/4 tsp (7 g) active dry yeast
- 1 1/2 tsp (9 g) salt

Instructions:

1. **Add Ingredients:** Pour warm milk, pumpkin puree, and olive oil into the bread machine pan. Add honey and salt.
2. **Add Flours and Veggies:** Add whole wheat flour, all-purpose flour, grated carrot, and yeast.
3. **Select Setting:** Choose the **Whole Wheat** setting and press Start.
4. **Monitor Dough:** Reduce liquid if needed; the dough should be slightly sticky.
5. **Bake:** Allow the bread machine to complete the cycle. Cool before slicing.

Expert Tips:

- **Vegetable Moisture:** Reduce other liquids slightly due to the moisture from pumpkin and carrot.
- **Even Grating:** Ensure carrot is finely grated for even distribution.

5.4 High-Fiber Bread

Cooking Time:
3 hours

Total Time:
3 hours 15 minutes

Preparation Time:
15 minutes

Nutritional Information (per 1 oz serving):

Calories: 130	**Carbohydrates:** 26 g	**Sodium:** 200 mg
Protein: 5 g	**Fat:** 3 g	**Sugars:** 3 g

Bread Machine Setting: Whole Wheat   **Quantity:** 1 loaf

Ingredients:

- 1 1/2 cups (360 ml) warm water
- 1/4 cup (60 ml) olive oil
- 2 tbsp (30 g) honey
- 2 cups (240 g) whole wheat flour

- 1 cup (120 g) oat bran
- 1/2 cup (60 g) flaxseed meal
- 2 1/4 tsp (7 g) active dry yeast
- 1 1/2 tsp (9 g) salt

Instructions:

1. **Add Ingredients:** Pour warm water, olive oil, and honey into the bread machine pan. Add salt.
2. **Add Flours and Fiber:** Add whole wheat flour, oat bran, flaxseed meal, and yeast.
3. **Select Setting:** Choose the **Whole Wheat** setting and press Start.
4. **Monitor Dough:** Increase water if necessary to achieve the right consistency.
5. **Bake:** Allow the bread machine to complete the cycle. Let cool before slicing.

Expert Tips:

- **Oat Bran and Flaxseed:** These high-fiber ingredients can absorb more moisture, so adjust as needed.
- **Texture Check:** Ensure dough is not too dry; add water gradually.

5.5 Protein-Added Bread

Preparation Time:	**Cooking Time:**	**Total Time:**
15 minutes	3 hours	3 hours 15 minutes

Nutritional Information (per 1 oz serving):

Calories: 140	**Carbohydrates:** 21 g	**Sodium:** 210 mg
Protein: 8 g	**Fat:** 4 g	**Sugars:** 4 g

Bread Machine Setting: Whole Wheat   **Quantity:** 1 loaf

Ingredients:

- 1 1/2 cups (360 ml) warm water
- 1/4 cup (60 ml) olive oil
- 2 tbsp (30 g) honey
- 2 cups (240 g) whole wheat flour

- 1/2 cup (60 g) pea protein powder
- 1/4 cup (30 g) cooked lentils
- 2 1/4 tsp (7 g) active dry yeast
- 1 1/2 tsp (9 g) salt

Instructions:

1. **Add Ingredients:** Pour warm water, olive oil, and honey into the bread machine pan. Add salt.
2. **Add Flours and Protein:** Add whole wheat flour, pea protein powder, cooked lentils, and yeast.
3. **Select Setting:** Choose the **Whole Wheat** setting and press Start.
4. **Monitor Dough:** Ensure consistency is manageable; adjust water if necessary.
5. **Bake:** Allow the bread machine to complete the cycle. Let cool before slicing.

Expert Tips:

- **Protein Powder:** Gradually incorporate to avoid clumps.
- **Lentils:** Make sure lentils are well-cooked and drained.

5.6 Healthy Fats Bread

Preparation Time:	**Cooking Time:**	**Total Time:**
15 minutes	3 hours	3 hours 15 minutes

Nutritional Information (per 1 oz serving):

Calories: 150	**Carbohydrates:** 22 g	**Sodium:** 210 mg
Protein: 5 g	**Fat:** 7 g	**Sugars:** 2 g

Bread Machine Setting: Whole Wheat   **Quantity:** 1 loaf

Ingredients:

- 1 1/2 cups (360 ml) warm water
- 1/4 cup (60 ml) olive oil
- 1/4 cup (60 g) mashed avocado
- 2 tbsp (30 g) honey
- 2 cups (240 g) whole wheat flour
- 1/2 cup (60 g) rolled oats
- 2 1/4 tsp (7 g) active dry yeast
- 1 1/2 tsp (9 g) salt

Instructions:

1. **Add Ingredients:** Pour warm water, olive oil, mashed avocado, and honey into the bread machine pan. Add salt.
2. **Add Flours and Oats:** Add whole wheat flour, rolled oats, and yeast.
3. **Select Setting:** Choose the **Whole Wheat** setting and press Start.
4. **Monitor Dough:** Adjust moisture with additional water if needed.
5. **Bake:** Allow the bread machine to complete the cycle. Cool before slicing.

Expert Tips:

- **Avocado Consistency:** Ensure avocado is fully mashed to avoid lumps.
- **Oats:** Can add extra texture and fiber.

5.7 Athletic Energy Bread

Preparation Time:
15 minutes

Cooking Time:
3 hours

Total Time:
3 hours 15 minutes

Nutritional Information (per 1 oz serving):

Calories: 160

Carbohydrates: 24 g

Sodium: 200 mg

Protein: 6 g

Fat: 5 g

Sugars: 5 g

Bread Machine Setting: Whole Wheat   **Quantity:** 1 loaf

Ingredients:

- 1 1/2 cups (360 ml) warm water
- 1/4 cup (60 ml) coconut oil
- 2 tbsp (30 g) honey
- 2 cups (240 g) whole wheat flour
- 1/2 cup (60 g) rolled oats
- 1/4 cup (30 g) dried fruit (e.g., raisins)
- 2 1/4 tsp (7 g) active dry yeast
- 1 1/2 tsp (9 g) salt

Instructions:

1. **Add Ingredients:** Pour warm water, coconut oil, and honey into the bread machine pan. Add salt.
2. **Add Flours and Extras:** Add whole wheat flour, rolled oats, dried fruit, and yeast.
3. **Select Setting:** Choose the **Whole Wheat** setting and press Start.
4. **Monitor Dough:** Adjust with additional water if the dough is too dry.
5. **Bake:** Allow the bread machine to complete the cycle. Cool before slicing.

Expert Tips:

- **Dried Fruit:** Can be soaked slightly in warm water to prevent burning.
- **Oats:** Provide slow-releasing energy.

5.8 Detox Bread

Preparation Time:
15 minutes

Cooking Time:
3 hours

Total Time:
3 hours 15 minutes

Nutritional Information (per 1 oz serving):

Calories: 130   **Carbohydrates:** 22 g   **Sodium:** 190 mg
Protein: 4 g   **Fat:** 3 g   **Sugars:** 2 g

Bread Machine Setting: Whole Wheat   **Quantity:** 1 loaf

Ingredients:

- 1 1/2 cups (360 ml) warm water
- 1/4 cup (60 ml) coconut oil
- 2 tbsp (30 g) honey
- 2 cups (240 g) whole wheat flour
- 1/2 cup (60 g) chia seeds
- 1/4 cup (30 g) spirulina powder
- 2 1/4 tsp (7 g) active dry yeast
- 1 1/2 tsp (9 g) salt

Instructions:

1. **Add Ingredients:** Pour warm water, coconut oil, and honey into the bread machine pan. Add salt.
2. **Add Flours and Detox Ingredients:** Add whole wheat flour, chia seeds, spirulina powder, and yeast.
3. **Select Setting:** Choose the **Whole Wheat** setting and press Start.
4. **Monitor Dough:** Adjust with additional water if needed.
5. **Bake:** Allow the bread machine to complete the cycle. Cool before slicing.

Expert Tips:

- **Spirulina:** A little goes a long way; ensure it is fully incorporated.
- **Chia Seeds:** Help with texture and add extra nutrients.

5.9 Diabetic-Friendly Bread

Preparation Time: **Cooking Time:**   **Total Time:**
15 minutes   3 hours   3 hours 15 minutes

Nutritional Information (per 1 oz serving):

Calories: 120   **Carbohydrates:** 18 g   **Sodium:** 200 mg
Protein: 6 g   **Fat:** 3 g   **Sugars:** 1 g

Bread Machine Setting: Whole Wheat   **Quantity:** 1 loaf

Ingredients:

- 1 1/2 cups (360 ml) warm water
- 1/4 cup (60 ml) olive oil
- 1/4 cup (60 g) erythritol (sugar substitute)

- 2 cups (240 g) almond flour
- 1/2 cup (60 g) flaxseed meal
- 2 1/4 tsp (7 g) active dry yeast
- 1 1/2 tsp (9 g) salt

Instructions:

1. **Add Ingredients:** Pour warm water, olive oil, and erythritol into the bread machine pan. Add salt.
2. **Add Flours:** Add almond flour, flaxseed meal, and yeast.
3. **Select Setting:** Choose the **Whole Wheat** setting and press Start.
4. **Monitor Dough:** Adjust moisture if necessary; almond flour absorbs differently.
5. **Bake:** Allow the bread machine to complete the cycle. Cool before slicing.

Expert Tips:

- **Erythritol:** Does not caramelize like sugar; ensure even mixing.
- **Moisture Check:** Almond flour can vary in moisture absorption.

5.10 Antioxidant-Rich Bread

Preparation Time:	Cooking Time:	Total Time:
15 minutes	3 hours	3 hours 15 minutes

Nutritional Information (per 1 oz serving):

Calories: 140	**Carbohydrates:** 21 g	**Sodium:** 210 mg
Protein: 5 g	**Fat:** 4 g	**Sugars:** 3 g

Bread Machine Setting: Whole Wheat   **Quantity:** 1 loaf

Ingredients:

- 1 1/2 cups (360 ml) warm water
- 1/4 cup (60 ml) olive oil
- 2 tbsp (30 g) honey
- 2 cups (240 g) whole wheat flour
- 1/4 cup (30 g) dried blueberries
- 1/4 cup (30 g) chopped dark chocolate (70% cocoa)
- 2 1/4 tsp (7 g) active dry yeast
- 1 1/2 tsp (9 g) salt

Instructions:

1. **Add Ingredients:** Pour warm water, olive oil, and honey into the bread machine pan. Add salt.
2. **Add Flours and Add-ins:** Add whole wheat flour, dried blueberries, chopped dark chocolate, and yeast.
3. **Select Setting:** Choose the **Whole Wheat** setting and press Start.

4. **Monitor Dough:** Adjust with additional water if needed for consistency.
5. **Bake:** Allow the bread machine to complete the cycle. Cool before slicing.

Expert Tips:

- **Blueberries:** Can be slightly soaked to avoid burning.
- **Chocolate:** Ensure even distribution for a consistent taste.

5.11 Herb and Spice Bread

Preparation Time:
10 minutes

Cooking Time:
3 hours

Total Time:
3 hours 10 minutes

Nutritional Information (per 1 oz serving):

Calories: 130

Carbohydrates: 23 g

Sodium: 210 mg

Protein: 5 g

Fat: 3 g

Sugars: 2 g

Bread Machine Setting: Whole Wheat

Quantity: 1 loaf

Ingredients:

- 1 1/2 cups (360 ml) warm water
- 1/4 cup (60 ml) olive oil
- 2 tbsp (30 g) honey
- 2 cups (240 g) whole wheat flour
- 1 tbsp (6 g) dried rosemary
- 1 tbsp (6 g) dried thyme
- 1 tsp (2 g) ground black pepper
- 2 1/4 tsp (7 g) active dry yeast
- 1 1/2 tsp (9 g) salt

Instructions:

1. **Add Ingredients:** Pour warm water, olive oil, and honey into the bread machine pan. Add salt.
2. **Add Flours and Seasonings:** Add whole wheat flour, dried rosemary, thyme, black pepper, and yeast.
3. **Select Setting:** Choose the **Whole Wheat** setting and press Start.
4. **Monitor Dough:** Adjust moisture if needed for consistency.
5. **Bake:** Allow the bread machine to complete the cycle. Cool before slicing.

Expert Tips:

- **Herbs:** Use fresh herbs for a stronger flavor if desired.
- **Pepper:** Adjust quantity to taste.

5.12 Sugar-Free Bread

Preparation Time:
10 minutes

Cooking Time:
3 hours

Total Time:
3 hours 10 minutes

Nutritional Information (per 1 oz serving):

Calories: 120

Carbohydrates: 22 g

Sodium: 200 mg

Protein: 6 g

Fat: 2 g

Sugars: 1 g

Bread Machine Setting: Whole Wheat

Quantity: 1 loaf

Ingredients:

- 1 1/2 cups (360 ml) warm water
- 1/4 cup (60 ml) coconut oil
- 1/4 cup (60 g) mashed ripe banana
- 2 cups (240 g) whole wheat flour
- 1/4 cup (30 g) chopped walnuts
- 2 1/4 tsp (7 g) active dry yeast
- 1 1/2 tsp (9 g) salt

Instructions:

1. **Add Ingredients:** Pour warm water, coconut oil, and mashed banana into the bread machine pan. Add salt.
2. **Add Flours and Add-ins:** Add whole wheat flour, chopped walnuts, and yeast.
3. **Select Setting:** Choose the **Whole Wheat** setting and press Start.
4. **Monitor Dough:** Adjust with additional water if needed.
5. **Bake:** Allow the bread machine to complete the cycle. Cool before slicing.

Expert Tips:

- **Banana:** Provides natural sweetness and moisture.
- **Walnuts:** Add texture and healthy fats.

5.13 Fermented Ingredient Bread

Preparation Time:
15 minutes

Cooking Time:
3 hours

Total Time:
3 hours 15 minutes

Nutritional Information (per 1 oz serving):

| **Calories:** 130 | **Carbohydrates:** 20 g | **Sodium:** 190 mg |
| **Protein:** 4 g | **Fat:** 3 g | **Sugars:** 3 g |

Bread Machine Setting: Whole Wheat   **Quantity:** 1 loaf

Ingredients:

- 1 1/2 cups (360 ml) warm kefir (or other fermented milk)
- 1/4 cup (60 ml) olive oil
- 2 tbsp (30 g) honey
- 2 cups (240 g) whole wheat flour
- 1/4 cup (30 g) finely chopped kimchi (drained)
- 2 1/4 tsp (7 g) active dry yeast
- 1 1/2 tsp (9 g) salt

Instructions:

1. **Add Ingredients:** Pour warm kefir, olive oil, and honey into the bread machine pan. Add salt.
2. **Add Flours and Kimchi:** Add whole wheat flour, chopped kimchi, and yeast.
3. **Select Setting:** Choose the **Whole Wheat** setting and press Start.
4. **Monitor Dough:** Adjust moisture if needed; kimchi may alter consistency.
5. **Bake:** Allow the bread machine to complete the cycle. Cool before slicing.

Expert Tips:

- **Kimchi:** Drained thoroughly to avoid excess moisture.
- **Kefir:** Adds probiotics; can be replaced with buttermilk if unavailable.

Chapter 6: Sourdough Bread

6.1 Introduction to Sourdough Starter

How to Prepare and Maintain Your Sourdough Starter

Preparation Time:
10 minutes

Fermentation Time:
5-7 days

Total Time:
7 days, 10 minutes

Quantity: 1 jar of starter (approximately 1 cup)

Ingredients:

- 1 cup (240 ml) warm water
- 1 cup (120 g) all-purpose flour

Instructions:

1. **Combine Ingredients:** In a clean jar, mix warm water with flour until well combined.
2. **Cover and Ferment:** Cover loosely with a lid or cloth and let sit at room temperature for 24 hours.
3. **Feed Starter:** Each day for 5-7 days, discard half of the starter, then add 1 cup (240 ml) warm water and 1 cup (120 g) flour. Mix well.
4. **Check for Bubbles:** The starter is ready when it is bubbly, has a pleasant sour smell, and has doubled in volume.

Expert Tips:

- **Consistency:** The starter should be thick and slightly bubbly. Adjust flour or water to maintain this consistency.
- **Temperature:** Keep the jar in a warm, draft-free area for optimal fermentation.

6.2 Classic Sourdough Bread

Preparation Time:
20 minutes

Cooking Time:
40 minutes

Total Time:
1 hour

Nutritional Information (per 1 oz serving):

Calories: 90
Protein: 3 g

Carbohydrates: 15 g
Fat: 0 g

Sodium: 200 mg
Sugars: 0 g

Bread Machine Setting: Dough (for mixing and first rise), Bake Only (for baking)
Quantity: 1 loaf

Ingredients:

- 1 cup (240 ml) warm water
- 1 cup (240 g) active sourdough starter
- 3 cups (360 g) all-purpose flour
- 1 1/2 tsp (8 g) salt

Instructions:

1. **Prepare Dough:** Add warm water and sourdough starter to the bread machine pan. Add flour and salt. Select the **Dough** setting and press Start.
2. **First Rise:** Allow the dough to rise in the machine for approximately 1 hour.
3. **Shape and Bake:** Transfer dough to a lightly floured surface and shape into a loaf. Place in the bread machine pan. Select the **Bake Only** setting and bake for 35-40 minutes.

Expert Tips:

- **Rise Time:** Ensure dough has doubled in size before starting the baking process.
- **Crust:** For a crispier crust, lightly mist the dough with water before baking.

6.3 Sourdough Bread with Seeds

Preparation Time: 20 minutes

Cooking Time: 40 minutes
Total Time: 1 hour

Nutritional Information (per 1 oz serving):

Calories: 100
Protein: 4 g

Carbohydrates: 15 g
Fat: 2 g

Sodium: 210 mg
Sugars: 0

Bread Machine Setting: Dough (for mixing and first rise), Bake Only (for baking)

Quantity: 1 loaf

Ingredients:

- 1 cup (240 ml) warm water
- 1 cup (240 g) active sourdough starter
- 3 cups (360 g) all-purpose flour
- 1 1/2 tsp (8 g) salt
- 1/4 cup (30 g) sunflower seeds
- 1/4 cup (30 g) sesame seeds

Instructions:

1. **Prepare Dough:** In the bread machine pan, combine warm water and sourdough starter. Add flour and salt. Select the **Dough** setting and press Start.
2. **Add Seeds:** When the machine beeps, add sunflower and sesame seeds.
3. **Shape and Bake:** Transfer dough to a lightly floured surface, shape into a loaf, and place in the bread machine pan. Select the **Bake Only** setting and bake for 35-40 minutes.

Expert Tips:

- **Seed Distribution:** Add seeds during the last 10 minutes of kneading to prevent them from getting crushed.
- **Hydration:** Adjust water if necessary as seeds can absorb moisture.

6.4 Sourdough Bread with Herbs

Preparation Time:	Cooking Time:	Total Time:
20 minutes	40 minutes	1 hour

Nutritional Information (per 1 oz serving):

Calories: 100	Carbohydrates: 15 g	Sodium: 210 mg
Protein: 3 g	Fat: 1 g	Sugars: 0 g

Bread Machine Setting: Dough (for mixing and first rise), Bake Only (for baking)
Quantity: 1 loaf

Ingredients:

- 1 cup (240 ml) warm water
- 1 cup (240 g) active sourdough starter
- 3 cups (360 g) all-purpose flour
- 1 1/2 tsp (8 g) salt
- 2 tbsp (6 g) dried rosemary
- 2 tbsp (6 g) dried thyme

Instructions:

1. **Prepare Dough:** Combine warm water and sourdough starter in the bread machine pan. Add flour, salt, rosemary, and thyme. Select the **Dough** setting and press Start.
2. **Shape and Bake:** Transfer dough to a lightly floured surface, shape into a loaf, and place in the bread machine pan. Select the **Bake Only** setting and bake for 35-40 minutes.

Expert Tips:

- **Herb Freshness:** Use dried herbs to ensure even distribution and prevent sogginess.
- **Flavor Balance:** Adjust the amount of herbs based on personal taste.

6.5 Sourdough Bread with Dried Fruit

Preparation Time:
20 minutes

Cooking Time:
45 minutes

Total Time:
1 hour 10 minutes

Nutritional Information (per 1 oz serving):

Calories: 110
Protein: 3 g

Carbohydrates: 18 g
Fat: 1 g

Sodium: 210 mg
Sugars: 6 g

Bread Machine Setting: Dough (for mixing and first rise), Bake Only (for baking)
Quantity: 1 loaf

Ingredients:

- 1 cup (240 ml) warm water
- 1 cup (240 g) active sourdough starter
- 3 cups (360 g) all-purpose flour

- 1 1/2 tsp (8 g) salt
- 1/2 cup (75 g) dried apricots, chopped
- 1/2 cup (75 g) dried cherries, chopped

Instructions:

1. **Prepare Dough:** Add warm water and sourdough starter to the bread machine pan. Add flour and salt. Select the **Dough** setting and press Start.
2. **Add Fruit:** When the machine beeps, add dried apricots and cherries.
3. **Shape and Bake:** Transfer dough to a lightly floured surface, shape into a loaf, and place in the bread machine pan. Select the **Bake Only** setting and bake for 40-45 minutes.

Expert Tips:

- **Rehydration:** Soak dried fruit in warm water for 10 minutes before adding to dough to prevent them from being too dry.
- **Even Distribution:** Add dried fruit during the last 10 minutes of kneading to keep pieces whole.

6.6 Sourdough Bread with Cheese

Preparation Time:
20 minutes

Cooking Time:
40 minutes

Total Time:
1 hour

Nutritional Information (per 1 oz serving):

Calories: 120
Protein: 5 g

Carbohydrates: 14 g
Fat: 4 g

Sodium: 300 mg
Sugars: 1 g

Bread Machine Setting: Dough (for mixing and first rise), Bake Only (for baking)
Quantity: 1 loaf

Ingredients:

- 1 cup (240 ml) warm water
- 1 cup (240 g) active sourdough starter
- 3 cups (360 g) all-purpose flour
- 1 1/2 tsp (8 g) salt
- 1/2 cup (60 g) shredded cheddar cheese

Instructions:

1. **Prepare Dough:** Combine warm water and sourdough starter in the bread machine pan. Add flour and salt. Select the **Dough** setting and press Start.
2. **Add Cheese:** When the machine beeps, add shredded cheddar cheese.
3. **Shape and Bake:** Transfer dough to a lightly floured surface, shape into a loaf, and place in the bread machine pan. Select the **Bake Only** setting and bake for 35-40 minutes.

Expert Tips:

- **Cheese Selection:** Use aged cheese for a more robust flavor.
- **Surface Cheese:** Sprinkle extra cheese on top of the dough before baking for a cheesy crust.

6.7 Sourdough Bread with Ancient Grains

Preparation Time:	Cooking Time:	Total Time:
20 minutes	45 minutes	1 hour 10 minutes

Nutritional Information (per 1 oz serving):

Calories: 100	**Carbohydrates:** 17 g	**Sodium:** 210 mg
Protein: 4 g	**Fat:** 1 g	**Sugars:** 1 g

Bread Machine Setting: Dough (for mixing and first rise), Bake Only (for baking)
Quantity: 1 loaf

Ingredients:

- 1 cup (240 ml) warm water
- 1 cup (240 g) active sourdough starter
- 2 cups (240 g) all-purpose flour
- 1 cup (120 g) ancient grain flour (e.g., spelt or farro)
- 1 1/2 tsp (8 g) salt

Instructions:

1. **Prepare Dough:** Add warm water and sourdough starter to the bread machine pan. Add all-purpose flour, ancient grain flour, and salt. Select the **Dough** setting and press Start.
2. **Shape and Bake:** Transfer dough to a lightly floured surface, shape into a loaf, and place in the bread machine pan. Select the **Bake Only** setting and bake for 40-45 minutes.

Expert Tips:

- **Grain Adjustment:** Ancient grains may require more water. Add a little extra water if the dough seems too dry.
- **Rise Time:** Allow for a slightly longer rising time if using a mix of flours.

6.8 Gluten-Free Sourdough Bread

Preparation Time:	**Cooking Time:**	**Total Time:**
20 minutes	50 minutes	1 hour 10 minutes

Nutritional Information (per 1 oz serving):

Calories: 110	**Carbohydrates:** 20 g	**Sodium:** 220 mg
Protein: 4 g	**Fat:** 2 g	**Sugars:** 2 g

Bread Machine Setting: Dough (for mixing and first rise), Bake Only (for baking)
Quantity: 1 loaf

Ingredients:

- 1 cup (240 ml) warm water
- 1 cup (240 g) active sourdough starter (gluten-free)
- 2 cups (240 g) gluten-free flour blend
- 1 cup (120 g) almond flour
- 1 1/2 tsp (8 g) salt
- 1 tsp (2 g) xanthan gum

Instructions:

1. **Prepare Dough:** Add warm water and sourdough starter to the bread machine pan. Add gluten-free flour blend, almond flour, salt, and xanthan gum. Select the **Dough** setting and press Start.
2. **Shape and Bake:** Transfer dough to a lightly floured surface, shape into a loaf, and place in the bread machine pan. Select the **Bake Only** setting and bake for 50 minutes.

Expert Tips:

- **Flour Blend:** Use a high-quality gluten-free flour blend for best results.
- **Texture:** Gluten-free dough may be stickier. Adjust flour blend if needed to achieve the right consistency.

6.9 Sourdough Bread with Spices

Preparation Time:
20 minutes

Cooking Time:
40 minutes

Total Time:
1 hour

Nutritional Information (per 1 oz serving):

Calories: 100

Carbohydrates: 15 g

Sodium: 210 mg

Protein: 3 g

Fat: 1 g

Sugars: 0 g

Bread Machine Setting: Dough (for mixing and first rise), Bake Only (for baking)
Quantity: 1 loaf

Ingredients:

- 1 cup (240 ml) warm water
- 1 cup (240 g) active sourdough starter
- 3 cups (360 g) all-purpose flour
- 1 1/2 tsp (8 g) salt
- 1 tsp (2 g) ground cinnamon
- 1/2 tsp (1 g) ground nutmeg

Instructions:

1. **Prepare Dough:** Combine warm water and sourdough starter in the bread machine pan. Add flour, salt, cinnamon, and nutmeg. Select the **Dough** setting and press Start.
2. **Shape and Bake:** Transfer dough to a lightly floured surface, shape into a loaf, and place in the bread machine pan. Select the **Bake Only** setting and bake for 35-40 minutes.

Expert Tips:

- **Spice Adjustment:** Adjust spice levels based on personal taste preferences.
- **Flavor Infusion:** For stronger spice flavor, increase the amount of spices slightly.

6.10 Sweet Sourdough Bread

Preparation Time:
20 minutes

Cooking Time:
45 minutes

Total Time:
1 hour 5 minutes

Nutritional Information (per 1 oz serving):

Calories: 120

Carbohydrates: 20 g

Sodium: 210 mg

Protein: 4 g

Fat: 2 g

Sugars: 8 g

Bread Machine Setting: Dough (for mixing and first rise), Bake Only (for baking)
Quantity: 1 loaf

Ingredients:

- 1 cup (240 ml) warm water
- 1 cup (240 g) active sourdough starter
- 3 cups (360 g) all-purpose flour
- 1 1/2 tsp (8 g) salt
- 1/4 cup (50 g) honey
- 1/2 cup (75 g) chocolate chips or dried fruit

Instructions:

1. **Prepare Dough:** Add warm water and sourdough starter to the bread machine pan. Add flour, salt, and honey. Select the **Dough** setting and press Start.
2. **Add Sweet Ingredients:** When the machine beeps, add chocolate chips or dried fruit.
3. **Shape and Bake:** Transfer dough to a lightly floured surface, shape into a loaf, and place in the bread machine pan. Select the **Bake Only** setting and bake for 45 minutes.

Expert Tips:

- **Sweet Additions:** Add sweet ingredients like chocolate chips during the last 10 minutes of kneading.
- **Moisture:** Adjust the amount of honey to ensure the dough is not too sticky.

Chapter 7: Sweet Breads

7.1 Cinnamon Sweet Bread

Preparation Time:
15 minutes

Cooking Time:
1 hour 20 minutes

Total Time:
1 hour 35 minutes

Nutritional Information (per 1 oz serving):

Calories: 110
Protein: 3 g

Carbohydrates: 18 g
Fat: 3 g

Sodium: 200 mg
Sugars: 8 g

Bread Machine Setting: Sweet Bread

Quantity: 1 loaf

Ingredients:

- 1 cup (240 ml) warm milk
- 1/4 cup (60 g) butter, softened
- 1/2 cup (100 g) granulated sugar
- 1 tsp (5 g) salt

- 2 1/4 tsp (7 g) active dry yeast
- 3 cups (360 g) all-purpose flour
- 2 tbsp (15 g) ground cinnamon

Instructions:

1. **Add Ingredients:** Place warm milk, softened butter, sugar, salt, and yeast into the bread machine pan. Let sit for 5 minutes to activate the yeast.
2. **Add Flour and Cinnamon:** Add flour and ground cinnamon. Select the **Sweet Bread** setting and press Start.
3. **Monitor Consistency:** Check the dough consistency after a few minutes of mixing. It should be smooth and elastic. Add more flour if necessary.
4. **Bake:** Allow the bread machine to complete the baking cycle. Let the bread cool before slicing.

Expert Tips:

- **Butter Addition:** Adding butter helps achieve a soft, tender crumb.

- **Cinnamon Distribution:** For even flavor, sprinkle cinnamon sugar mixture over the dough before baking.

7.2 Sweet Fruit Bread

Preparation Time:
20 minutes

Cooking Time:
1 hour 30 minutes

Total Time:
1 hour 50 minutes

Nutritional Information (per 1 oz serving):

Calories: 120

Protein: 4 g

Carbohydrates: 21 g

Fat: 3 g

Sodium: 210 mg

Sugars: 10 g

Bread Machine Setting: Sweet Bread

Quantity: 1 loaf

Ingredients:

- 1 cup (240 ml) warm milk
- 1/4 cup (60 g) butter, softened
- 1/2 cup (100 g) granulated sugar
- 1 tsp (5 g) salt

- 2 1/4 tsp (7 g) active dry yeast
- 3 cups (360 g) all-purpose flour
- 1 cup (150 g) mixed dried fruit (raisins, chopped apples)

Instructions:

1. **Combine Ingredients:** Pour warm milk, softened butter, sugar, salt, and yeast into the bread machine pan. Allow the yeast to activate for 5 minutes.
2. **Add Flour and Fruit:** Add flour and mixed dried fruit. Select the **Sweet Bread** setting and press Start.
3. **Add Fruit:** If your machine has an audible signal for add-ins, add fruit when prompted.
4. **Bake:** Let the bread machine complete the baking cycle. Cool before slicing.

Expert Tips:

- **Fruit Hydration:** Soak dried fruit in warm water for 10 minutes to prevent it from becoming too dry.
- **Moisture Balance:** Adjust flour if the dough seems too wet due to the added fruit.

7.3 Chocolate Sweet Bread

Preparation Time:	**Cooking Time:**	**Total Time:**
15 minutes	1 hour 30 minutes	1 hour 45 minutes

Nutritional Information (per 1 oz serving):

Calories: 130	**Carbohydrates:** 20 g	**Sodium:** 220 mg
Protein: 4 g	**Fat:** 4 g	**Sugars:** 12

Bread Machine Setting: Sweet Bread   **Quantity:** 1 loaf

Ingredients:

- 1 cup (240 ml) warm milk
- 1/4 cup (60 g) butter, softened
- 1/2 cup (100 g) granulated sugar
- 1 tsp (5 g) salt
- 2 1/4 tsp (7 g) active dry yeast
- 2 1/2 cups (300 g) all-purpose flour
- 1/2 cup (90 g) semi-sweet chocolate chips

Instructions:

1. **Prepare Ingredients:** Add warm milk, butter, sugar, salt, and yeast to the bread machine pan. Let the yeast activate for 5 minutes.
2. **Add Flour and Chocolate:** Add flour and chocolate chips. Select the **Sweet Bread** setting and press Start.
3. **Monitor Dough:** Ensure the chocolate chips are evenly distributed throughout the dough.
4. **Bake:** Allow the bread machine to complete the baking cycle. Cool before slicing.

Expert Tips:

- **Chocolate Quality:** Use high-quality chocolate chips for a richer flavor.
- **Avoid Burning:** If you notice the chocolate starting to burn, reduce the baking time slightly.

7.4 Honey Sweet Bread

Preparation Time:	**Cooking Time:**	**Total Time:**
15 minutes	1 hour 20 minutes	1 hour 35 minutes

Nutritional Information (per 1 oz serving):

| **Calories:** 120 | **Carbohydrates:** 20 g | **Sodium:** 200 mg |
| **Protein:** 3 g | **Fat:** 3 g | **Sugars:** 10 |

Bread Machine Setting: Sweet Bread   **Quantity:** 1 loaf

Ingredients:

- 1 cup (240 ml) warm milk
- 1/4 cup (60 g) butter, softened
- 1/2 cup (100 g) honey
- 1 tsp (5 g) salt
- 2 1/4 tsp (7 g) active dry yeast
- 3 cups (360 g) all-purpose flour

Instructions:

1. **Combine Ingredients:** Place warm milk, softened butter, honey, salt, and yeast in the bread machine pan. Let the yeast activate for 5 minutes.
2. **Add Flour:** Add flour. Select the **Sweet Bread** setting and press Start.
3. **Bake:** Allow the machine to complete the baking cycle. For a golden crust, brush the top of the loaf with honey before baking.

Expert Tips:

- **Honey Application:** Brushing with honey helps create a glossy, golden crust.
- **Sweet Balance:** Adjust honey amount if the bread is too sweet for your taste.

7.5 Sweet Bread with Nuts and Seeds

| **Preparation Time:** | **Cooking Time:** | **Total Time:** |
| 20 minutes | 1 hour 30 minutes | 1 hour 50 minutes |

Nutritional Information (per 1 oz serving):

| **Calories:** 130 | **Carbohydrates:** 19 g | **Sodium:** 220 mg |
| **Protein:** 4 g | **Fat:** 5 g | **Sugars:** 7 g |

Bread Machine Setting: Sweet Bread   **Quantity:** 1 loaf

Ingredients:

- 1 cup (240 ml) warm milk
- 1/4 cup (60 g) butter, softened
- 1/2 cup (100 g) granulated sugar
- 1 tsp (5 g) salt
- 2 1/4 tsp (7 g) active dry yeast
- 2 1/2 cups (300 g) all-purpose flour
- 1/4 cup (30 g) sunflower seeds
- 1/4 cup (30 g) chopped walnuts

Instructions:

1. **Prepare Ingredients:** Add warm milk, butter, sugar, salt, and yeast to the bread machine pan. Allow the yeast to activate for 5 minutes.
2. **Add Flour and Nuts:** Add flour, sunflower seeds, and chopped walnuts. Select the **Sweet Bread** setting and press Start.
3. **Add Nuts:** If your machine signals for add-ins, add nuts and seeds when prompted.
4. **Bake:** Let the machine complete the baking cycle. Cool before slicing.

Expert Tips:

- **Nut Crunch:** Adding nuts towards the end of the mixing cycle helps retain their crunchiness.
- **Fat Balance:** Use butter or oil to keep the bread moist and tender.

7.6 Vanilla Sweet Bread

Preparation Time:	**Cooking Time:**	**Total Time:**
15 minutes	1 hour 20 minutes	1 hour 35 minutes

Nutritional Information (per 1 oz serving):

Calories: 110	**Carbohydrates:** 18 g	**Sodium:** 200 mg
Protein: 3 g	**Fat:** 3 g	**Sugars:** 9 g

Bread Machine Setting: Sweet Bread
Quantity: 1 loaf

Ingredients:

- 1 cup (240 ml) warm milk
- 1/4 cup (60 g) butter, softened
- 1/2 cup (100 g) granulated sugar
- 1 tsp (5 g) salt
- 2 1/4 tsp (7 g) active dry yeast
- 3 cups (360 g) all-purpose flour
- 1 tbsp (15 ml) vanilla extract

Instructions:

1. **Combine Ingredients:** Pour warm milk, butter, sugar, salt, and yeast into the bread machine pan. Allow the yeast to activate for 5 minutes.
2. **Add Flour and Vanilla:** Add flour and vanilla extract. Select the **Sweet Bread** setting and press Start.
3. **Bake:** Let the bread machine complete the baking cycle. Allow the bread to cool before slicing.

Expert Tips:

- **Vanilla Quality:** Use high-quality vanilla extract for a richer flavor.
- **Soft Texture:** Adding milk powder helps achieve a softer texture.

7.7 Strawberry Sweet Bread

Preparation Time:	Cooking Time:	Total Time:
20 minutes	1 hour 30 minutes	1 hour 50 minutes

Nutritional Information (per 1 oz serving):

Calories: 120	**Carbohydrates:** 21 g	**Sodium:** 210 mg
Protein: 3 g	**Fat:** 3 g	**Sugars:** 11 g

Bread Machine Setting: Sweet Bread   **Quantity:** 1 loaf

Ingredients:

- 1 cup (240 ml) warm milk
- 1/4 cup (60 g) butter, softened
- 1/2 cup (100 g) granulated sugar
- 1 tsp (5 g) salt
- 2 1/4 tsp (7 g) active dry yeast
- 3 cups (360 g) all-purpose flour
- 1 cup (150 g) chopped fresh strawberries (tossed with 1 tbsp flour)

Instructions:

1. **Prepare Ingredients:** Add warm milk, butter, sugar, salt, and yeast to the bread machine pan. Let the yeast activate for 5 minutes.
2. **Add Flour and Strawberries:** Add flour and chopped strawberries. Select the **Sweet Bread** setting and press Start.
3. **Add Strawberries:** If your machine has an audible signal for add-ins, add strawberries when prompted.
4. **Bake:** Let the bread machine complete the baking cycle. Cool before slicing.

Expert Tips:

- **Strawberry Moisture:** Toss strawberries in flour to prevent them from making the dough too wet.
- **Fruit Freshness:** Use fresh strawberries for a brighter flavor.

7.8 Jam Sweet Bread

Preparation Time:
20 minutes

Cooking Time:
1 hour 30 minutes

Total Time:
1 hour 50 minutes

Nutritional Information (per 1 oz serving):

Calories: 130
Protein: 4 g

Carbohydrates: 22 g
Fat: 3 g

Sodium: 220 mg
Sugars: 12 g

Bread Machine Setting: Sweet Bread   **Quantity:** 1 loaf

Ingredients:

- 1 cup (240 ml) warm milk
- 1/4 cup (60 g) butter, softened
- 1/2 cup (100 g) granulated sugar
- 1 tsp (5 g) salt

- 2 1/4 tsp (7 g) active dry yeast
- 2 1/2 cups (300 g) all-purpose flour
- 1/2 cup (150 g) fruit jam (your choice)

Instructions:

1. **Combine Ingredients:** Place warm milk, butter, sugar, salt, and yeast into the bread machine pan. Let yeast activate for 5 minutes.
2. **Add Flour:** Add flour. Select the **Sweet Bread** setting and press Start.
3. **Add Jam:** When the dough is nearly done mixing, add the jam to the center of the dough.
4. **Bake:** Allow the machine to complete the baking cycle. Let the bread cool before slicing.

Expert Tips:

- **Jam Placement:** Place jam in the center to avoid it burning on the edges.
- **Baking Time:** If the jam starts to ooze out, reduce baking time slightly.

7.9 Almond Sweet Bread

Preparation Time:
20 minutes

Cooking Time:
1 hour 30 minutes

Total Time:
1 hour 50 minutes

Nutritional Information (per 1 oz serving):

Calories: 130
Protein: 4 g

Carbohydrates: 19 g
Fat: 5 g

Sodium: 220 mg
Sugars: 8 g

Bread Machine Setting: Sweet Bread   **Quantity:** 1 loaf

Ingredients:

- 1 cup (240 ml) warm milk
- 1/4 cup (60 g) butter, softened
- 1/2 cup (100 g) granulated sugar
- 1 tsp (5 g) salt

- 2 1/4 tsp (7 g) active dry yeast
- 2 1/2 cups (300 g) all-purpose flour
- 1/4 cup (30 g) chopped almonds
- 1/2 tsp (2 ml) almond extract

Instructions:

1. **Combine Ingredients:** Pour warm milk, butter, sugar, salt, and yeast into the bread machine pan. Let yeast activate for 5 minutes.
2. **Add Flour and Almonds:** Add flour, chopped almonds, and almond extract. Select the **Sweet Bread** setting and press Start.
3. **Bake:** Allow the bread machine to complete the baking cycle. Cool before slicing.

Expert Tips:

- **Almond Extract:** Use a high-quality almond extract for a stronger flavor.
- **Nut Placement:** Add nuts towards the end of the mixing cycle to maintain their crunch.

7.10 Spiced Sweet Bread

Preparation Time:	**Cooking Time:**	**Total Time:**
15 minutes	1 hour 20 minutes	1 hour 35 minutes

Nutritional Information (per 1 oz serving):

Calories: 120	**Carbohydrates:** 20 g	**Sodium:** 210 mg
Protein: 3 g	**Fat:** 3 g	**Sugars:** 9 g

Bread Machine Setting: Sweet Bread   **Quantity:** 1 loaf

Ingredients:

- 1 cup (240 ml) warm milk
- 1/4 cup (60 g) butter, softened
- 1/2 cup (100 g) granulated sugar
- 1 tsp (5 g) salt

- 2 1/4 tsp (7 g) active dry yeast
- 3 cups (360 g) all-purpose flour
- 1 tsp (2 g) ground cinnamon
- 1/2 tsp (1 g) ground cloves

Instructions:

1. **Combine Ingredients:** Add warm milk, butter, sugar, salt, and yeast to the bread machine pan. Let yeast activate for 5 minutes.

2. **Add Flour and Spices:** Add flour, cinnamon, and cloves. Select the **Sweet Bread** setting and press Start.
3. **Bake:** Allow the bread machine to complete the baking cycle. Let the bread cool before slicing.

Expert Tips:

- **Spice Mixing:** Combine spices with the flour for even distribution.
- **Sugar and Spice:** Adjust the sugar and spice levels to taste for a more customized flavor.

Chapter 8: Vegan Bread

8.1 Classic Vegan Bread

Preparation Time:	**Cooking Time:**	**Total Time:**
15 minutes	30 minutes	45 minutes

Nutritional Information (per slice, 1 oz):

Calories: 130	**Carbohydrates:** 23 g	**Sodium:** 200 mg
Protein: 4 g	**Fat:** 2 g	**Sugars:** 2 g

Bread Machine Setting: Basic   **Quantity:** 1 loaf

Ingredients:

- 1 cup (240 ml) warm water
- 1/4 cup (60 ml) vegetable oil
- 1/4 cup (50 g) maple syrup
- 2 1/4 tsp (7 g) active dry yeast
- 3 1/2 cups (420 g) all-purpose flour
- 1 tsp (6 g) salt

Instructions:

1. **Combine Wet Ingredients:** In the bread machine pan, combine warm water, vegetable oil, and maple syrup. Sprinkle yeast over the mixture and let sit for 5 minutes.
2. **Add Dry Ingredients:** Add flour and salt to the pan.
3. **Mix and Knead:** Select the **Basic** setting and press Start. The machine will mix, knead, and let the dough rise.
4. **Bake:** Once the dough cycle is complete, shape if necessary and place it back in the pan. Select the **Basic** setting for baking.
5. **Cool:** Remove the bread from the pan and cool on a wire rack before slicing.

Expert Tips:

- **Consistency Check:** Ensure the dough is not too sticky. If it is, add a little more flour, one tablespoon at a time.
- **Oil Substitution:** You can substitute vegetable oil with other plant-based oils, like olive oil, for a different flavor.

8.2 Vegan Bread with Seeds and Nuts

Preparation Time:	**Cooking Time:**	**Total Time:**
20 minutes	35 minutes	55 minutes

Nutritional Information (per slice, 1 oz):

Calories: 150	**Carbohydrates:** 26 g	**Sodium:** 210 mg
Protein: 5 g	**Fat:** 5 g	**Sugars:** 2 g

Bread Machine Setting: Basic   **Quantity:** 1 loaf

Ingredients:

- 1 cup (240 ml) warm water
- 1/4 cup (60 ml) olive oil
- 1/4 cup (50 g) agave syrup
- 2 1/4 tsp (7 g) active dry yeast
- 3 cups (360 g) whole wheat flour
- 1/2 cup (60 g) sunflower seeds
- 1/2 cup (60 g) chopped walnuts
- 1 tsp (6 g) salt

Instructions:

1. **Prepare Wet Ingredients:** Combine warm water, olive oil, and agave syrup in the bread machine pan. Sprinkle yeast over the mixture and let sit for 5 minutes.
2. **Add Dry Ingredients:** Add whole wheat flour and salt to the pan.
3. **Mix and Knead:** Select the **Basic** setting and press Start. The machine will handle mixing, kneading, and rising.
4. **Add Seeds and Nuts:** When the machine beeps to add additional ingredients, add sunflower seeds and chopped walnuts.
5. **Bake:** Once the dough cycle completes, shape if necessary and place the dough in the pan. Select the **Basic** setting for baking.
6. **Cool:** Cool the bread on a wire rack before slicing.

Expert Tips:

- **Seed Toasting:** Lightly toast seeds and nuts before adding them for enhanced flavor.
- **Ingredient Distribution:** Make sure seeds and nuts are evenly distributed throughout the dough.

8.3 Vegan Chocolate Bread

Preparation Time: 20 minutes

Cooking Time: 35 minutes
Total Time: 55 minutes

Nutritional Information (per slice, 1 oz):

Calories: 160	**Carbohydrates:** 26 g	**Sodium:** 210 mg
Protein: 4 g	**Fat:** 5 g	**Sugars:** 15 g

Bread Machine Setting: Basic

Quantity: 1 loaf

Ingredients:

- 1 cup (240 ml) warm water
- 1/4 cup (60 ml) vegetable oil
- 1/4 cup (50 g) brown sugar
- 2 1/4 tsp (7 g) active dry yeast
- 3 cups (360 g) all-purpose flour
- 1/2 cup (50 g) unsweetened cocoa powder
- 1 tsp (6 g) salt

- 1/2 cup (90 g) dairy-free chocolate chips

Instructions:

1. **Combine Wet Ingredients:** In the bread machine pan, mix warm water, vegetable oil, and brown sugar. Sprinkle yeast over the mixture and let sit for 5 minutes.
2. **Add Dry Ingredients:** Add flour, cocoa powder, and salt to the pan.
3. **Mix and Knead:** Select the **Basic** setting and press Start. The machine will mix, knead, and rise the dough.
4. **Add Chocolate Chips:** Add chocolate chips when the machine beeps to add additional ingredients.
5. **Bake:** Once the dough cycle completes, shape if needed and place it in the pan. Select the **Basic** setting for baking.
6. **Cool:** Let the bread cool on a wire rack before slicing.

Expert Tips:

- **Cocoa Quality:** Use high-quality cocoa powder for a richer chocolate flavor.
- **Chip Distribution:** Fold chocolate chips in gently to prevent them from sinking to the bottom.

8.4 Vegan Herb Bread

Preparation Time:	Cooking Time:	Total Time:
15 minutes	30 minutes	45 minutes

Nutritional Information (per slice, 1 oz):

Calories: 140	Carbohydrates: 24 g	Sodium: 200 mg
Protein: 4 g	Fat: 3 g	Sugars: 2 g

Bread Machine Setting: Basic   **Quantity:** 1 loaf

Ingredients:

- 1 cup (240 ml) warm water
- 1/4 cup (60 ml) olive oil
- 1/4 cup (50 g) maple syrup
- 2 1/4 tsp (7 g) active dry yeast
- 3 1/2 cups (420 g) all-purpose flour
- 1 tsp (6 g) salt
- 2 tbsp (8 g) dried mixed herbs (e.g., rosemary, thyme, basil)

Instructions:

1. **Combine Wet Ingredients:** Mix warm water, olive oil, and maple syrup in the bread machine pan. Sprinkle yeast over the mixture and let sit for 5 minutes.

2. **Add Dry Ingredients:** Add flour, salt, and dried herbs to the pan.
3. **Mix and Knead:** Select the **Basic** setting and press Start. The machine will handle mixing, kneading, and rising.
4. **Bake:** Once the dough cycle is complete, shape if necessary and place it back in the pan. Select the **Basic** setting for baking.
5. **Cool:** Cool on a wire rack before slicing.

Expert Tips:

*   **Herb Freshness:** Use fresh or well-preserved dried herbs for the best flavor.
*   **Herb Mixing:** Adjust herb quantities based on personal taste preferences.

8.5 Vegan Fruit Bread

Preparation Time:	**Cooking Time:**	**Total Time:**
20 minutes	35 minutes	55 minutes

Nutritional Information (per slice, 1 oz):

Calories: 150	**Carbohydrates:** 25 g	**Sodium:** 200 mg
Protein: 4 g	**Fat:** 4 g	**Sugars:** 12

Bread Machine Setting: Basic   **Quantity:** 1 loaf

Ingredients:

*   1 cup (240 ml) warm water
*   1/4 cup (60 ml) vegetable oil
*   1/4 cup (50 g) agave syrup
*   2 1/4 tsp (7 g) active dry yeast
*   3 cups (360 g) all-purpose flour
*   1 tsp (6 g) salt
*   1/2 cup (75 g) chopped dried fruit (e.g., apricots, raisins)

Instructions:

1. **Prepare Wet Ingredients:** Combine warm water, vegetable oil, and agave syrup in the bread machine pan. Sprinkle yeast over the mixture and let sit for 5 minutes.
2. **Add Dry Ingredients:** Add flour and salt to the pan.
3. **Mix and Knead:** Select the **Basic** setting and press Start. The machine will mix, knead, and let the dough rise.
4. **Add Dried Fruit:** Add chopped dried fruit when the machine beeps to add additional ingredients.

5. **Bake:** Once the dough cycle is complete, shape if necessary and place it back in the pan. Select the **Basic** setting for baking.
6. **Cool:** Cool on a wire rack before slicing.

Expert Tips:

- **Fruit Quality:** Use high-quality dried fruit for the best flavor and texture.
- **Moisture Balance:** Ensure the fruit is well-dried to avoid excess moisture in the dough.

8.6 Vegan Spiced Bread

Preparation Time:
20 minutes

Cooking Time:
35 minutes

Total Time:
55 minutes

Nutritional Information (per slice, 1 oz):

Calories: 160

Carbohydrates: 27 g

Sodium: 210 mg

Protein: 4 g

Fat: 4 g

Sugars: 12 g

Bread Machine Setting: Basic

Quantity: 1 loaf

Ingredients:

- 1 cup (240 ml) warm water
- 1/4 cup (60 ml) olive oil
- 1/4 cup (50 g) brown sugar
- 2 1/4 tsp (7 g) active dry yeast

- 3 1/2 cups (420 g) all-purpose flour
- 1 tsp (6 g) salt
- 1 tsp (4 g) ground cinnamon
- 1/2 tsp (1 g) ground nutmeg

Instructions:

1. **Combine Wet Ingredients:** Mix warm water, olive oil, and brown sugar in the bread machine pan. Sprinkle yeast over the mixture and let sit for 5 minutes.
2. **Add Dry Ingredients:** Add flour, salt, cinnamon, and nutmeg to the pan.
3. **Mix and Knead:** Select the **Basic** setting and press Start. The machine will handle mixing, kneading, and rising.
4. **Bake:** Once the dough cycle is complete, shape if needed and place it back in the pan. Select the **Basic** setting for baking.
5. **Cool:** Cool on a wire rack before slicing.

Expert Tips:

- **Spice Adjustments:** Adjust spice levels based on personal preferences.
- **Storage:** Store in an airtight container to keep the bread fresh.

8.7 Vegan Alternative Flour Bread

Preparation Time:	**Cooking Time:**	**Total Time:**
20 minutes	35 minutes	55 minutes

Nutritional Information (per slice, 1 oz):

Calories: 150	**Carbohydrates:** 25 g	**Sodium:** 200 mg
Protein: 5 g	**Fat:** 4 g	**Sugars:** 3 g

Bread Machine Setting: Basic   **Quantity:** 1 loaf

Ingredients:

- 1 cup (240 ml) warm water
- 1/4 cup (60 ml) coconut oil
- 1/4 cup (50 g) maple syrup
- 2 1/4 tsp (7 g) active dry yeast
- 2 cups (240 g) almond flour
- 1 cup (120 g) oat flour
- 1 tsp (6 g) salt

Instructions:

1. **Prepare Wet Ingredients:** Mix warm water, coconut oil, and maple syrup in the bread machine pan. Sprinkle yeast over the mixture and let sit for 5 minutes.
2. **Add Dry Ingredients:** Add almond flour, oat flour, and salt to the pan.
3. **Mix and Knead:** Select the **Basic** setting and press Start. The machine will mix, knead, and rise the dough.
4. **Bake:** Once the dough cycle completes, shape if necessary and place it back in the pan. Select the **Basic** setting for baking.
5. **Cool:** Cool on a wire rack before slicing.

Expert Tips:

- **Flour Blending:** Ensure the blend of flours is well-mixed to maintain a consistent texture.
- **Storage:** Store in a cool, dry place to prevent spoilage.

Chapter 9: Gluten-Free Bread

9.1 Classic Gluten-Free Bread

Preparation Time: 15 minutes

Cooking Time: 40 minutes
Total Time: 55 minutes

Nutritional Information (per slice, 1 oz):

Calories: 140
Protein: 3 g

Carbohydrates: 25 g
Fat: 3 g

Sodium: 210 mg
Sugars: 3 g

Bread Machine Setting: Gluten-Free

Quantity: 1 loaf

Ingredients:

- 1 1/2 cups (360 ml) warm water
- 1/4 cup (60 ml) vegetable oil
- 1/4 cup (50 g) honey
- 2 1/4 tsp (7 g) gluten-free active dry yeast

- 3 cups (360 g) gluten-free all-purpose flour blend
- 1/4 cup (30 g) potato starch
- 1 tsp (6 g) xanthan gum
- 1 tsp (6 g) salt

Instructions:

1. **Combine Wet Ingredients:** In the bread machine pan, mix warm water, vegetable oil, and honey. Sprinkle yeast over the mixture and let sit for 5 minutes.
2. **Add Dry Ingredients:** Add gluten-free flour blend, potato starch, xanthan gum, and salt.
3. **Mix and Knead:** Select the **Gluten-Free** setting and press Start. The machine will handle mixing, kneading, and rising.
4. **Bake:** Once the dough cycle completes, select the **Bake** setting and bake until golden brown.
5. **Cool:** Remove the bread from the pan and cool on a wire rack before slicing.

Expert Tips:

- **Texture Check:** Ensure your gluten-free flour blend includes xanthan gum or guar gum for the best texture.
- **Cool Before Slicing:** Allow the bread to cool completely before slicing to avoid crumbling.

9.2 Gluten-Free Bread with Seeds

Preparation Time:	Cooking Time:	Total Time:
20 minutes	40 minutes	1 hour

Nutritional Information (per slice, 1 oz):

Calories: 160	**Carbohydrates:** 26 g	**Sodium:** 220 mg
Protein: 4 g	**Fat:** 5 g	**Sugars:** 3 g

Bread Machine Setting: Gluten-Free   **Quantity:** 1 loaf

Ingredients:

- 1 1/2 cups (360 ml) warm water
- 1/4 cup (60 ml) olive oil
- 1/4 cup (50 g) maple syrup
- 2 1/4 tsp (7 g) gluten-free active dry yeast
- 3 cups (360 g) gluten-free all-purpose flour blend
- 1/4 cup (30 g) chia seeds
- 1/4 cup (30 g) sunflower seeds
- 1 tsp (6 g) xanthan gum
- 1 tsp (6 g) salt

Instructions:

1. **Combine Wet Ingredients:** In the bread machine pan, mix warm water, olive oil, and maple syrup. Sprinkle yeast over the mixture and let sit for 5 minutes.
2. **Add Dry Ingredients:** Add gluten-free flour blend, chia seeds, sunflower seeds, xanthan gum, and salt.
3. **Mix and Knead:** Select the **Gluten-Free** setting and press Start. The machine will mix, knead, and rise the dough.
4. **Bake:** Once the dough cycle is complete, select the **Bake** setting and bake until golden brown.
5. **Cool:** Cool on a wire rack before slicing.

Expert Tips:

- **Seed Freshness:** Use fresh seeds for the best flavor and texture.
- **Mix Thoroughly:** Ensure seeds are evenly distributed throughout the dough.

9.3 Gluten-Free Bread with Alternative Flours

Preparation Time:	Cooking Time:	Total Time:
20 minutes	45 minutes	1 hour 5 minutes

Nutritional Information (per slice, 1 oz):

Calories: 150	**Carbohydrates:** 24 g	**Sodium:** 210 mg
Protein: 4 g	**Fat:** 4 g	**Sugars:** 2 g

Bread Machine Setting: Gluten-Free   **Quantity:** 1 loaf

Ingredients:

- 1 cup (240 ml) warm water
- 1/4 cup (60 ml) coconut oil
- 1/4 cup (50 g) agave syrup
- 2 1/4 tsp (7 g) gluten-free active dry yeast
- 1 cup (120 g) almond flour
- 1 cup (120 g) oat flour
- 1 1/2 cups (180 g) gluten-free all-purpose flour blend
- 1 tsp (6 g) xanthan gum
- 1 tsp (6 g) salt

Instructions:

1. **Combine Wet Ingredients:** Mix warm water, coconut oil, and agave syrup in the bread machine pan. Sprinkle yeast over the mixture and let sit for 5 minutes.
2. **Add Dry Ingredients:** Add almond flour, oat flour, gluten-free flour blend, xanthan gum, and salt.
3. **Mix and Knead:** Select the **Gluten-Free** setting and press Start. The machine will mix, knead, and rise the dough.
4. **Bake:** Once the dough cycle is complete, select the **Bake** setting and bake until golden brown.
5. **Cool:** Cool on a wire rack before slicing.

Expert Tips:

- **Flour Blending:** Adjust flour types to achieve the desired texture and flavor.
- **Monitor Consistency:** The dough should be thick and slightly sticky.

9.4 Gluten-Free Bread with Fruit

Preparation Time:	**Cooking Time:**	**Total Time:**
20 minutes	40 minutes	1 hour

Nutritional Information (per slice, 1 oz):

Calories: 160	**Carbohydrates:** 27 g	**Sodium:** 210 mg
Protein: 4 g	**Fat:** 4 g	**Sugars:** 10 g

Bread Machine Setting: Gluten-Free   **Quantity:** 1 loaf

Ingredients:

- 1 1/2 cups (360 ml) warm water
- 1/4 cup (60 ml) vegetable oil
- 1/4 cup (50 g) honey
- 2 1/4 tsp (7 g) gluten-free active dry yeast
- 3 cups (360 g) gluten-free all-purpose flour blend
- 1/2 cup (75 g) chopped dried fruit (e.g., apricots, raisins)
- 1 tsp (6 g) xanthan gum
- 1 tsp (6 g) salt

Instructions:

1. **Combine Wet Ingredients:** In the bread machine pan, mix warm water, vegetable oil, and honey. Sprinkle yeast over the mixture and let sit for 5 minutes.
2. **Add Dry Ingredients:** Add gluten-free flour blend, xanthan gum, and salt.
3. **Add Dried Fruit:** Add chopped dried fruit when the machine beeps to add additional ingredients.
4. **Mix and Knead:** Select the **Gluten-Free** setting and press Start. The machine will handle mixing, kneading, and rising.
5. **Bake:** Once the dough cycle completes, select the **Bake** setting and bake until golden brown.
6. **Cool:** Cool on a wire rack before slicing.

Expert Tips:

- **Fruit Quality:** Use high-quality dried fruit for better flavor.
- **Even Distribution:** Ensure fruit is evenly distributed to prevent uneven texture.

9.5 Gluten-Free Bread with Herbs

Preparation Time:	Cooking Time:	Total Time:
20 minutes	40 minutes	1 hour

Nutritional Information (per slice, 1 oz):

Calories: 150	**Carbohydrates:** 25 g	**Sodium:** 210 mg
Protein: 4 g	**Fat:** 4 g	**Sugars:** 3 g

Bread Machine Setting: Gluten-Free   **Quantity:** 1 loaf

Ingredients:

- 1 1/2 cups (360 ml) warm water
- 1/4 cup (60 ml) olive oil
- 1/4 cup (50 g) agave syrup

- 2 1/4 tsp (7 g) gluten-free active dry yeast
- 3 cups (360 g) gluten-free all-purpose flour blend
- 2 tbsp (8 g) dried mixed herbs (e.g., rosemary, thyme)
- 1 tsp (6 g) xanthan gum
- 1 tsp (6 g) salt

Instructions:

1. **Combine Wet Ingredients:** Mix warm water, olive oil, and agave syrup in the bread machine pan. Sprinkle yeast over the mixture and let sit for 5 minutes.
2. **Add Dry Ingredients:** Add gluten-free flour blend, dried herbs, xanthan gum, and salt.
3. **Mix and Knead:** Select the **Gluten-Free** setting and press Start. The machine will handle mixing, kneading, and rising.
4. **Bake:** Once the dough cycle is complete, select the **Bake** setting and bake until golden brown.
5. **Cool:** Cool on a wire rack before slicing.

Expert Tips:

- **Herb Freshness:** Use fresh or well-preserved dried herbs for the best flavor.
- **Flavor Balance:** Adjust herb quantities to suit your taste preferences.

9.6 Classic Gluten-Free Bread

Preparation Time:
15 minutes

Cooking Time:
60 minutes

Total Time:
1 hour 15 minutes

Nutritional Information (per slice, 1 oz):

Calories: 150

Carbohydrates: 30 g

Sodium: 280 mg

Protein: 3 g

Fat: 2 g

Sugars: 2 g

Bread Machine Setting: Basic

Quantity: 1 loaf

Ingredients:

- 1 1/2 cups (360 ml) warm water
- 1/4 cup (60 ml) vegetable oil
- 2 tbsp (30 g) honey
- 1/4 cup (30 g) gluten-free flour blend (e.g., rice flour, tapioca flour)
- 2 1/4 tsp (7 g) active dry yeast
- 3 cups (360 g) gluten-free all-purpose flour
- 1 1/2 tsp (9 g) salt
- 1 tbsp (7 g) xanthan gum

Instructions:

1. **Combine Ingredients:** In the bread machine pan, mix warm water, vegetable oil, and honey. Sprinkle yeast over the mixture and let sit for 5 minutes.
2. **Add Dry Ingredients:** Add gluten-free flour blend, gluten-free all-purpose flour, salt, and xanthan gum.
3. **Mix and Knead:** Select the **Basic** setting and press Start. The machine will mix, knead, and rise the dough.
4. **Bake:** Once the dough cycle completes, select the **Bake** setting and bake until golden brown.
5. **Cool:** Allow the bread to cool on a wire rack before slicing.

Expert Tips:

- **Xanthan Gum:** Essential for adding elasticity to gluten-free dough, ensuring a better texture.
- **Cool Completely:** Gluten-free bread needs to cool fully to set properly and slice without crumbling.

9.7 Gluten-Free Bread with Cheese

Preparation Time:	**Cooking Time:** 6	**Total Time:**
15 minutes	0 minutes	1 hour 15 minutes

Nutritional Information (per slice, 1 oz):

Calories: 180	**Carbohydrates:** 30 g	**Sodium:** 320 mg
Protein: 6 g	**Fat:** 5 g	**Sugars:** 1 g

Bread Machine Setting: Basic   **Quantity:** 1 loaf

Ingredients:

- 1 1/2 cups (360 ml) warm water
- 1/4 cup (60 ml) vegetable oil
- 2 tbsp (30 g) honey
- 1/4 cup (30 g) gluten-free flour blend
- 2 1/4 tsp (7 g) active dry yeast
- 3 cups (360 g) gluten-free all-purpose flour
- 1 1/2 tsp (9 g) salt
- 1 cup (120 g) shredded cheese (e.g., cheddar, mozzarella)
- 1 tbsp (7 g) xanthan gum

Instructions:

1. **Combine Ingredients:** In the bread machine pan, mix warm water, vegetable oil, and honey. Sprinkle yeast over the mixture and let sit for 5 minutes.
2. **Add Dry Ingredients:** Add gluten-free flour blend, gluten-free all-purpose flour, salt, xanthan gum, and shredded cheese.
3. **Mix and Knead:** Select the **Basic** setting and press Start. The machine will mix, knead, and rise the dough.
4. **Bake:** Once the dough cycle completes, select the **Bake** setting and bake until golden brown.
5. **Cool:** Allow the bread to cool on a wire rack before slicing.

Expert Tips:

- **Cheese Type:** Choose a cheese with good melting qualities for a rich flavor.
- **Cool Completely:** This helps avoid a gummy texture in the bread.

9.8 Gluten-Free Sandwich Bread

Preparation Time:	**Cooking Time:**	**Total Time:**
15 minutes	60 minutes	1 hour 15 minutes

Nutritional Information (per slice, 1 oz):

Calories: 160	**Carbohydrates:** 30 g	**Sodium:** 300 mg
Protein: 4 g	**Fat:** 2 g	**Sugars:** 2 g

Bread Machine Setting: Basic   **Quantity:** 1 loaf

Ingredients:

- 1 1/2 cups (360 ml) warm water
- 1/4 cup (60 ml) vegetable oil
- 2 tbsp (30 g) sugar
- 2 1/4 tsp (7 g) active dry yeast
- 3 1/2 cups (420 g) gluten-free all-purpose flour
- 1 1/2 tsp (9 g) salt
- 1 tbsp (7 g) xanthan gum

Instructions:

1. **Combine Ingredients:** In the bread machine pan, mix warm water, vegetable oil, and sugar. Sprinkle yeast over the mixture and let sit for 5 minutes.
2. **Add Dry Ingredients:** Add gluten-free all-purpose flour, salt, and xanthan gum.

3. **Mix and Knead:** Select the **Basic** setting and press Start. The machine will mix, knead, and rise the dough.
4. **Bake:** Once the dough cycle completes, select the **Bake** setting and bake until golden brown.
5. **Cool:** Allow the bread to cool on a wire rack before slicing.

Expert Tips:

- **Texture:** For the best sandwich bread texture, ensure your dough is slightly thick but not dry.
- **Slice Evenly:** Allow the bread to cool completely to make slicing easier and to achieve neat, even slices.

9.9 Gluten-Free Spiced Bread

Preparation Time:
15 minutes

Cooking Time:
60 minutes

Total Time:
1 hour 15 minutes

Nutritional Information (per slice, 1 oz):

Calories: 170

Carbohydrates: 31 g

Sodium: 300 mg

Protein: 4 g

Fat: 2 g

Sugars: 4 g

Bread Machine Setting: Basic

Quantity: 1 loaf

Ingredients:

- 1 1/2 cups (360 ml) warm water
- 1/4 cup (60 ml) vegetable oil
- 2 tbsp (30 g) brown sugar
- 2 1/4 tsp (7 g) active dry yeast
- 3 1/2 cups (420 g) gluten-free all-purpose flour

- 1 1/2 tsp (9 g) salt
- 2 tsp (4 g) ground cinnamon
- 1 tsp (2 g) ground ginger
- 1 tbsp (7 g) xanthan gum

Instructions:

1. **Combine Ingredients:** In the bread machine pan, mix warm water, vegetable oil, and brown sugar. Sprinkle yeast over the mixture and let sit for 5 minutes.
2. **Add Dry Ingredients:** Add gluten-free all-purpose flour, salt, ground cinnamon, ground ginger, and xanthan gum.
3. **Mix and Knead:** Select the **Basic** setting and press Start. The machine will mix, knead, and rise the dough.
4. **Bake:** Once the dough cycle completes, select the **Bake** setting and bake until golden brown.

5. **Cool:** Allow the bread to cool on a wire rack before slicing.

Expert Tips:

- **Spice Freshness:** Use fresh ground spices for the most vibrant flavor.
- **Even Mixing:** Ensure spices are well mixed with the flour for consistent flavor throughout.

9.10 Gluten-Free Bread with Superfoods

Preparation Time:	**Cooking Time:**	**Total Time:**
15 minutes	60 minutes	1 hour 15 minutes

Nutritional Information (per slice, 1 oz):

Calories: 170	**Carbohydrates:** 28 g	**Sodium:** 290 mg
Protein: 5 g	**Fat:** 4 g	**Sugars:** 3 g

Bread Machine Setting: Basic   **Quantity:** 1 loaf

Ingredients:

- 1 1/2 cups (360 ml) warm water
- 1/4 cup (60 ml) vegetable oil
- 2 tbsp (30 g) honey
- 2 1/4 tsp (7 g) active dry yeast
- 3 cups (360 g) gluten-free all-purpose flour
- 1/2 cup (60 g) chia seeds
- 1/2 cup (60 g) flaxseeds
- 1 1/2 tsp (9 g) salt
- 1 tbsp (7 g) xanthan gum

Instructions:

1. **Combine Ingredients:** In the bread machine pan, mix warm water, vegetable oil, and honey. Sprinkle yeast over the mixture and let sit for 5 minutes.
2. **Add Dry Ingredients:** Add gluten-free all-purpose flour, chia seeds, flaxseeds, salt, and xanthan gum.
3. **Mix and Knead:** Select the **Basic** setting and press Start. The machine will mix, knead, and rise the dough.
4. **Bake:** Once the dough cycle completes, select the **Bake** setting and bake until golden brown.
5. **Cool:** Allow the bread to cool on a wire rack before slicing.

Expert Tips:

- **Superfood Quality:** Use fresh chia and flaxseeds for maximum nutritional benefit.

- **Seed Distribution:** Ensure seeds are evenly distributed throughout the dough for consistent texture and nutrition.

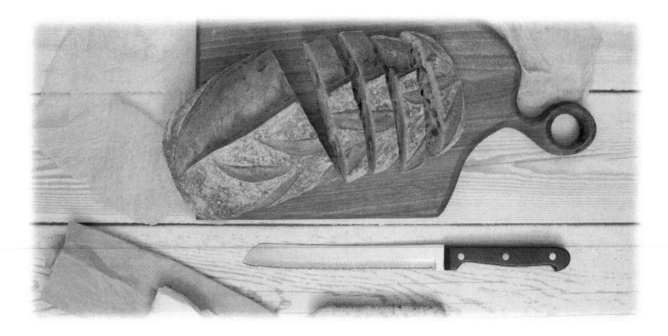

Chapter 10: Keto Bread

10.1 Classic Keto Bread

Preparation Time:
10 minutes

Cooking Time:
60 minutes

Total Time:
1 hour 10 minutes

Nutritional Information (per slice, 1 oz):

Calories: 180
Protein: 8 g

Carbohydrates: 5 g
Fat: 14 g

Sodium: 320 mg
Sugars: 1 g

Bread Machine Setting: Basic

Quantity: 1 loaf

Ingredients:

- 1 cup (240 ml) warm water
- 1/4 cup (60 ml) olive oil
- 1 tbsp (15 g) apple cider vinegar
- 2 tbsp (14 g) vital wheat gluten
- 2 cups (200 g) almond flour

- 1/2 cup (50 g) flaxseed meal
- 1/4 cup (30 g) psyllium husk
- 1 tbsp (7 g) xanthan gum
- 2 tsp (6 g) baking powder
- 2 large eggs

- 1 tsp (5 g) salt
- 2 1/4 tsp (7 g) active dry yeast

Instructions:

1. **Combine Ingredients:** In the bread machine pan, mix warm water, olive oil, and apple cider vinegar. Sprinkle yeast over the mixture and let sit for 5 minutes.
2. **Add Dry Ingredients:** Add vital wheat gluten, almond flour, flaxseed meal, psyllium husk, xanthan gum, baking powder, eggs, and salt.
3. **Mix and Knead:** Select the **Basic** setting and press Start. The machine will mix, knead, and rise the dough.
4. **Bake:** Once the dough cycle completes, select the **Bake** setting and bake until golden brown.
5. **Cool:** Allow the bread to cool on a wire rack before slicing.

Expert Tips:

- **Consistency:** Ensure all ingredients are well mixed to achieve a uniform texture.
- **Cool Completely:** This helps the bread set properly and prevents it from being gummy.

10.2 Keto Bread with Seeds

Preparation Time:
10 minutes

Cooking Time:
60 minutes

Total Time:
1 hour 10 minutes

Nutritional Information (per slice, 1 oz):

Calories: 190

Carbohydrates: 6 g

Sodium: 330 mg

Protein: 8 g

Fat: 15 g

Sugars: 1 g

Bread Machine Setting: Basic

Quantity: 1 loaf

Ingredients:

- 1 cup (240 ml) warm water
- 1/4 cup (60 ml) olive oil
- 1 tbsp (15 g) apple cider vinegar
- 2 tbsp (14 g) vital wheat gluten
- 1 cup (100 g) almond flour
- 1/2 cup (50 g) flaxseed meal
- 1/4 cup (30 g) chia seeds
- 1/4 cup (30 g) sunflower seeds
- 1 tbsp (7 g) xanthan gum
- 2 tsp (6 g) baking powder
- 2 large eggs
- 1 tsp (5 g) salt
- 2 1/4 tsp (7 g) active dry yeast

Instructions:

1. **Combine Ingredients:** In the bread machine pan, mix warm water, olive oil, and apple cider vinegar. Sprinkle yeast over the mixture and let sit for 5 minutes.
2. **Add Dry Ingredients:** Add vital wheat gluten, almond flour, flaxseed meal, chia seeds, sunflower seeds, xanthan gum, baking powder, eggs, and salt.
3. **Mix and Knead:** Select the **Basic** setting and press Start. The machine will mix, knead, and rise the dough.
4. **Bake:** Once the dough cycle completes, select the **Bake** setting and bake until golden brown.
5. **Cool:** Allow the bread to cool on a wire rack before slicing.

Expert Tips:

- **Seed Freshness:** Use fresh seeds for the best texture and flavor.
- **Mix Evenly:** Ensure seeds are well incorporated to avoid clumping.

10.3 Keto Bread with Cheese

Preparation Time:
10 minutes

Cooking Time:
60 minutes

Total Time:
1 hour 10 minutes

Nutritional Information (per slice, 1 oz):

Calories: 200
Protein: 10 g

Carbohydrates: 5 g
Fat: 16 g

Sodium: 350 mg
Sugars: 1 g

Bread Machine Setting: Basic

Quantity: 1 loaf

Ingredients:

- 1 cup (240 ml) warm water
- 1/4 cup (60 ml) olive oil
- 1 tbsp (15 g) apple cider vinegar
- 2 tbsp (14 g) vital wheat gluten
- 1 cup (100 g) almond flour
- 1/2 cup (50 g) flaxseed meal

- 1 cup (100 g) shredded cheddar cheese
- 1 tbsp (7 g) xanthan gum
- 2 tsp (6 g) baking powder
- 2 large eggs
- 1 tsp (5 g) salt
- 2 1/4 tsp (7 g) active dry yeast

Instructions:

1. **Combine Ingredients:** In the bread machine pan, mix warm water, olive oil, and apple cider vinegar. Sprinkle yeast over the mixture and let sit for 5 minutes.
2. **Add Dry Ingredients:** Add vital wheat gluten, almond flour, flaxseed meal, shredded cheddar cheese, xanthan gum, baking powder, eggs, and salt.
3. **Mix and Knead:** Select the **Basic** setting and press Start. The machine will mix, knead, and rise the dough.

4. **Bake:** Once the dough cycle completes, select the **Bake** setting and bake until golden brown.
5. **Cool:** Allow the bread to cool on a wire rack before slicing.

Expert Tips:

- **Cheese Selection:** Choose a cheese that melts well for a rich flavor.
- **Cool Fully:** Helps achieve the best texture and prevents a gummy center.

10.4 Keto Bread with Herbs

Preparation Time:	Cooking Time:	Total Time:
10 minutes	60 minutes	1 hour 10 minutes

Nutritional Information (per slice, 1 oz):

Calories: 170	**Carbohydrates:** 6 g	**Sodium:** 300 mg
Protein: 8 g	**Fat:** 13 g	**Sugars:** 1 g

Bread Machine Setting: Basic   **Quantity:** 1 loaf

Ingredients:

- 1 cup (240 ml) warm water
- 1/4 cup (60 ml) olive oil
- 1 tbsp (15 g) apple cider vinegar
- 2 tbsp (14 g) vital wheat gluten
- 2 cups (200 g) almond flour
- 1/2 cup (50 g) flaxseed meal
- 1 tbsp (5 g) dried rosemary
- 1 tbsp (5 g) dried thyme
- 1 tbsp (7 g) xanthan gum
- 2 tsp (6 g) baking powder
- 2 large eggs
- 1 tsp (5 g) salt
- 2 1/4 tsp (7 g) active dry yeas

Instructions:

1. **Combine Ingredients:** In the bread machine pan, mix warm water, olive oil, and apple cider vinegar. Sprinkle yeast over the mixture and let sit for 5 minutes.
2. **Add Dry Ingredients:** Add vital wheat gluten, almond flour, flaxseed meal, dried rosemary, dried thyme, xanthan gum, baking powder, eggs, and salt.
3. **Mix and Knead:** Select the **Basic** setting and press Start. The machine will mix, knead, and rise the dough.
4. **Bake:** Once the dough cycle completes, select the **Bake** setting and bake until golden brown.
5. **Cool:** Allow the bread to cool on a wire rack before slicing.

Expert Tips:

- **Herb Freshness:** Use fresh or high-quality dried herbs for the best flavor.
- **Even Mixing:** Ensure herbs are evenly distributed to avoid clumps of flavor.

10.5 Keto Sweet Bread

Preparation Time:
10 minutes

Cooking Time:
60 minutes

Total Time:
1 hour 10 minutes

Nutritional Information (per slice, 1 oz):

Calories: 190
Protein: 8 g

Carbohydrates: 7 g
Fat: 14 g

Sodium: 310 mg
Sugars: 2 g

Bread Machine Setting: Basic

Quantity: 1 loaf

Ingredients:

- 1 cup (240 ml) warm water
- 1/4 cup (60 ml) coconut oil
- 2 tbsp (30 g) erythritol or keto-friendly sweetener
- 2 tbsp (14 g) vital wheat gluten
- 2 cups (200 g) almond flour
- 1/2 cup (50 g) flaxseed meal
- 1 tsp (5 g) ground cinnamon
- 1/2 tsp (2 g) ground nutmeg
- 1 tbsp (7 g) xanthan gum
- 2 tsp (6 g) baking powder
- 2 large eggs
- 1 tsp (5 g) salt
- 2 1/4 tsp (7 g) active dry yeast

Instructions:

1. **Combine Ingredients:** In the bread machine pan, mix warm water, coconut oil, and erythritol. Sprinkle yeast over the mixture and let sit for 5 minutes.
2. **Add Dry Ingredients:** Add vital wheat gluten, almond flour, flaxseed meal, ground cinnamon, ground nutmeg, xanthan gum, baking powder, eggs, and salt.
3. **Mix and Knead:** Select the **Basic** setting and press Start. The machine will mix, knead, and rise the dough.
4. **Bake:** Once the dough cycle completes, select the **Bake** setting and bake until golden brown.
5. **Cool:** Allow the bread to cool on a wire rack before slicing.

Expert Tips:

- **Sweetener Choice:** Adjust the sweetener based on personal preference and sweetness level desired.
- **Even Spice Distribution:** Ensure spices are well mixed to avoid uneven flavor.

10.6 Keto Bread with Fruit

Preparation Time:	**Cooking Time:**	**Total Time:**
10 minutes	60 minutes	1 hour 10 minutes

Nutritional Information (per slice, 1 oz):

Calories: 190	**Carbohydrates:** 8 g	**Sodium:** 320 mg
Protein: 8 g	**Fat:** 14 g	**Sugars:** 2 g

Bread Machine Setting: Basic   **Quantity:** 1 loaf

Ingredients:

- 1 cup (240 ml) warm water
- 1/4 cup (60 ml) coconut oil
- 2 tbsp (30 g) erythritol or keto-friendly sweetener
- 2 tbsp (14 g) vital wheat gluten
- 2 cups (200 g) almond flour
- 1/2 cup (50 g) flaxseed meal
- 1/2 cup (70 g) unsweetened dried blueberries, chopped
- 1 tbsp (7 g) xanthan gum
- 2 tsp (6 g) baking powder
- 2 large eggs
- 1 tsp (5 g) salt
- 2 1/4 tsp (7 g) active dry yeast

Instructions:

1. **Combine Ingredients:** In the bread machine pan, mix warm water, coconut oil, and erythritol. Sprinkle yeast over the mixture and let sit for 5 minutes.
2. **Add Dry Ingredients:** Add vital wheat gluten, almond flour, flaxseed meal, dried blueberries, xanthan gum, baking powder, eggs, and salt.
3. **Mix and Knead:** Select the **Basic** setting and press Start. The machine will mix, knead, and rise the dough.
4. **Bake:** Once the dough cycle completes, select the **Bake** setting and bake until golden brown.
5. **Cool:** Allow the bread to cool on a wire rack before slicing.

Expert Tips:

- **Fruit Preparation:** Chop dried fruit into small pieces to evenly distribute throughout the bread.
- **Cooling:** Ensure the bread cools fully to prevent a gummy texture.

10.7 Keto Bread with Spices

Preparation Time:	**Cooking Time:**	**Total Time:**
10 minutes	60 minutes	1 hour 10 minutes

Nutritional Information (per slice, 1 oz):

Calories: 180	**Carbohydrates:** 6 g	**Sodium:** 310 mg
Protein: 8 g	**Fat:** 14 g	**Sugars:** 1 g

Bread Machine Setting: Basic   **Quantity:** 1 loaf

Ingredients:

- 1 cup (240 ml) warm water
- 1/4 cup (60 ml) olive oil
- 2 tbsp (30 g) erythritol or keto-friendly sweetener
- 2 tbsp (14 g) vital wheat gluten
- 2 cups (200 g) almond flour
- 1/2 cup (50 g) flaxseed meal
- 1 tbsp (7 g) ground cinnamon
- 1/2 tsp (2 g) ground cloves
- 1/2 tsp (2 g) ground nutmeg
- 1 tbsp (7 g) xanthan gum
- 2 tsp (6 g) baking powder
- 2 large eggs
- 1 tsp (5 g) salt
- 2 1/4 tsp (7 g) active dry yeast

Instructions:

1. **Combine Ingredients:** In the bread machine pan, mix warm water, olive oil, and erythritol. Sprinkle yeast over the mixture and let sit for 5 minutes.
2. **Add Dry Ingredients:** Add vital wheat gluten, almond flour, flaxseed meal, ground cinnamon, ground cloves, ground nutmeg, xanthan gum, baking powder, eggs, and salt.
3. **Mix and Knead:** Select the **Basic** setting and press Start. The machine will mix, knead, and rise the dough.
4. **Bake:** Once the dough cycle completes, select the **Bake** setting and bake until golden brown.
5. **Cool:** Allow the bread to cool on a wire rack before slicing.

Expert Tips:

- **Spice Freshness:** Use freshly ground spices for the best flavor.
- **Even Mixing:** Ensure spices are evenly distributed to avoid clumps of intense flavor.

10.8 Keto Bread with Alternative Flours

Preparation Time:
10 minutes

Cooking Time:
60 minutes

Total Time:
1 hour 10 minutes

Nutritional Information (per slice, 1 oz):

Calories: 180
Protein: 8 g

Carbohydrates: 6 g
Fat: 14 g

Sodium: 320 mg
Sugars: 1 g

Bread Machine Setting: Basic

Quantity: 1 loaf

Ingredients:

- 1 cup (240 ml) warm water
- 1/4 cup (60 ml) coconut oil
- 2 tbsp (30 g) erythritol or keto-friendly sweetener
- 2 tbsp (14 g) vital wheat gluten
- 1 cup (100 g) almond flour
- 1 cup (100 g) coconut flour

- 1/2 cup (50 g) flaxseed meal
- 1 tbsp (7 g) xanthan gum
- 2 tsp (6 g) baking powder
- 2 large eggs
- 1 tsp (5 g) salt
- 2 1/4 tsp (7 g) active dry yeast

Instructions:

1. **Combine Ingredients:** In the bread machine pan, mix warm water, coconut oil, and erythritol. Sprinkle yeast over the mixture and let sit for 5 minutes.
2. **Add Dry Ingredients:** Add vital wheat gluten, almond flour, coconut flour, flaxseed meal, xanthan gum, baking powder, eggs, and salt.
3. **Mix and Knead:** Select the **Basic** setting and press Start. The machine will mix, knead, and rise the dough.
4. **Bake:** Once the dough cycle completes, select the **Bake** setting and bake until golden brown.
5. **Cool:** Allow the bread to cool on a wire rack before slicing.

Expert Tips:

- **Flour Blending:** Ensure a good blend of almond and coconut flour for optimal texture.
- **Check Consistency:** The dough should be thick but not dry. Adjust with a little extra water if needed.

10.9 Keto Bread for Sandwiches

Preparation Time:
10 minutes

Cooking Time:
60 minutes

Total Time:
1 hour 10 minutes

Nutritional Information (per slice, 1 oz):

| **Calories:** 180 | **Carbohydrates:** 5 g | **Sodium:** 320 mg |
| **Protein:** 8 g | **Fat:** 14 g | **Sugars:** 1 g |

Bread Machine Setting: Basic   **Quantity:** 1 loaf

Ingredients:

- 1 cup (240 ml) warm water
- 1/4 cup (60 ml) olive oil
- 2 tbsp (30 g) erythritol or keto-friendly sweetener
- 2 tbsp (14 g) vital wheat gluten
- 2 cups (200 g) almond flour
- 1/2 cup (50 g) flaxseed meal
- 1 tbsp (7 g) xanthan gum
- 2 tsp (6 g) baking powder
- 2 large eggs
- 1 tsp (5 g) salt
- 2 1/4 tsp (7 g) active dry yeast

Instructions:

1. **Combine Ingredients:** In the bread machine pan, mix warm water, olive oil, and erythritol. Sprinkle yeast over the mixture and let sit for 5 minutes.
2. **Add Dry Ingredients:** Add vital wheat gluten, almond flour, flaxseed meal, xanthan gum, baking powder, eggs, and salt.
3. **Mix and Knead:** Select the **Basic** setting and press Start. The machine will mix, knead, and rise the dough.
4. **Bake:** Once the dough cycle completes, select the **Bake** setting and bake until golden brown.
5. **Cool:** Allow the bread to cool on a wire rack before slicing.

Expert Tips:

- **Slice Thickness:** For sandwich bread, slice evenly for the best presentation and ease of use.
- **Cooling:** Ensure full cooling before slicing to avoid squished or gummy bread.

10.10 Keto Bread with Superfoods

| **Preparation Time:** | **Cooking Time:** | **Total Time:** |
| 10 minutes | 60 minutes | 1 hour 10 minutes |

Nutritional Information (per slice, 1 oz):

| **Calories:** 190 | **Carbohydrates:** 7 g | **Sodium:** 330 mg |
| **Protein:** 8 g | **Fat:** 15 g | **Sugars:** 1 g |

Bread Machine Setting: Basic   **Quantity:** 1 loaf

Ingredients:

- 1 cup (240 ml) warm water
- 1/4 cup (60 ml) olive oil
- 2 tbsp (30 g) erythritol or keto-friendly sweetener
- 2 tbsp (14 g) vital wheat gluten
- 2 cups (200 g) almond flour
- 1/2 cup (50 g) flaxseed meal
- 2 tbsp (15 g) chia seeds
- 2 tbsp (15 g) hemp seeds
- 1 tbsp (7 g) xanthan gum
- 2 tsp (6 g) baking powder
- 2 large eggs
- 1 tsp (5 g) salt
- 2 1/4 tsp (7 g) active dry yeast

Instructions:

1. **Combine Ingredients:** In the bread machine pan, mix warm water, olive oil, and erythritol. Sprinkle yeast over the mixture and let sit for 5 minutes.
2. **Add Dry Ingredients:** Add vital wheat gluten, almond flour, flaxseed meal, chia seeds, hemp seeds, xanthan gum, baking powder, eggs, and salt.
3. **Mix and Knead:** Select the **Basic** setting and press Start. The machine will mix, knead, and rise the dough.
4. **Bake:** Once the dough cycle completes, select the **Bake** setting and bake until golden brown.
5. **Cool:** Allow the bread to cool on a wire rack before slicing.

Expert Tips:

- **Superfood Freshness:** Use fresh chia and hemp seeds for maximum nutritional benefits.
- **Even Distribution:** Ensure even mixing of seeds to avoid clumping.

Chapter 11: Beyond Bread

11.1 Pizza Dough

Preparation Time:	**Cooking Time:**	**Total Time:**
10 minutes	1 hour	1 hour 10 minutes

Nutritional Information (per 1 oz serving):

Calories: 120	**Carbohydrates:** 22 g	**Sodium:** 230 mg
Protein: 4 g	**Fat:** 2 g	**Sugars:** 1 g

Bread Machine Setting: Dough	**Quantity:** 1 pizza crust

Ingredients:

- 1 cup (240 ml) warm water
- 2 tbsp (30 ml) olive oil
- 2 tbsp (30 g) honey or sugar
-
- 2 1/4 tsp (7 g) active dry yeast
- 2 1/2 cups (300 g) all-purpose flour
- 1 tsp (5 g) salt

Instructions:

1. **Prepare the Yeast Mixture:** In the bread machine pan, combine warm water, olive oil, and honey. Sprinkle yeast over the top and let sit for 5 minutes.
2. **Add Dry Ingredients:** Add flour and salt to the pan.
3. **Mix and Knead:** Select the **Dough** setting and press Start. The machine will mix and knead the dough.
4. **First Rise:** Let the dough rise in the pan for about 30 minutes or until doubled in size.
5. **Shape and Pre-Bake:** Remove the dough, roll it out to your desired thickness, and pre-bake at 450°F (230°C) for 5-7 minutes.
6. **Add Toppings and Bake:** Add your favorite toppings and bake for an additional 10-15 minutes.

Expert Tips:

- **Non-Sticky Dough:** Use flour to dust your rolling surface to prevent sticking.
- **Crispy Crust:** Pre-bake the crust before adding toppings for a crispier result.

11.2 Focaccia Dough

Preparation Time:	Cooking Time:	Total Time:
15 minutes	1 hour	1 hour 15 minutes

Nutritional Information (per 1 oz serving):

Calories: 150	**Carbohydrates:** 22 g	**Sodium:** 250 mg
Protein: 4 g	**Fat:** 5 g	**Sugars:** 1 g

Bread Machine Setting: Dough   **Quantity:** 1 focaccia

Ingredients:

- 1 1/2 cups (360 ml) warm water
- 1/4 cup (60 ml) olive oil
- 2 tsp (10 g) sugar
- 2 1/4 tsp (7 g) active dry yeast
- 4 cups (500 g) all-purpose flour
- 1 tbsp (15 g) salt
- Fresh rosemary and sea salt for topping

Instructions:

1. **Prepare the Yeast Mixture:** In the bread machine pan, mix warm water, olive oil, and sugar. Sprinkle yeast over and let sit for 5 minutes.
2. **Add Dry Ingredients:** Add flour and salt to the pan.
3. **Mix and Knead:** Select the **Dough** setting and press Start. The machine will mix and knead the dough.
4. **First Rise:** Let the dough rise in the pan for about 1 hour or until doubled in size.
5. **Shape and Bake:** Transfer to a greased baking sheet, dimple with your fingers, and top with rosemary and sea salt. Bake at 425°F (220°C) for 20-25 minutes.

Expert Tips:

- **Dimpling the Dough:** Use your fingers to create dimples in the dough for an authentic focaccia texture.
- **Season Generously:** Don't skimp on olive oil and sea salt for maximum flavor.

11.3 Brioche Dough

Preparation Time:
15 minutes

Cooking Time:
1 hour 30 minutes

Total Time:
1 hour 45 minutes

Nutritional Information (per 1 oz serving):

Calories: 180
Protein: 5 g

Carbohydrates: 22 g
Fat: 8 g

Sodium: 180 mg
Sugars: 6 g

Bread Machine Setting: Dough

Quantity: 1 loaf

Ingredients:

- 1/2 cup (120 ml) warm milk
- 1/2 cup (120 ml) melted butter
- 1/2 cup (100 g) sugar
- 4 large eggs

- 3 cups (360 g) all-purpose flour
- 1/4 cup (30 g) vital wheat gluten
- 2 1/4 tsp (7 g) active dry yeast
- 1 tsp (5 g) salt

Instructions:

1. **Combine Ingredients:** In the bread machine pan, mix warm milk, melted butter, and sugar. Add yeast and let sit for 5 minutes.
2. **Add Dry Ingredients:** Add flour, vital wheat gluten, eggs, and salt.
3. **Mix and Knead:** Select the **Dough** setting and press Start. The machine will mix and knead the dough.
4. **First Rise:** Let the dough rise in the pan for about 1 hour or until doubled.
5. **Shape and Second Rise:** Shape the dough into a loaf, place in a greased pan, and let rise for another 30 minutes.
6. **Bake:** Bake at 375°F (190°C) for 25-30 minutes or until golden brown.

Expert Tips:

- **Butter Handling:** Ensure butter is well incorporated for a rich texture.
- **Second Rise:** Allow adequate rising time for a soft, fluffy brioche.

11.4 Hot Dog and Hamburger Buns Dough

Preparation Time:
10 minutes

Cooking Time:
1 hour

Total Time:
1 hour 10 minutes

Nutritional Information (per 1 oz serving):

Calories: 150
Protein: 5 g

Carbohydrates: 25 g
Fat: 2 g

Sodium: 250 mg
Sugars: 2 g

Bread Machine Setting: Dough

Quantity: 8 buns

Ingredients:

- 1 cup (240 ml) warm milk
- 1/4 cup (60 ml) vegetable oil
- 2 tbsp (30 g) sugar

- 2 1/4 tsp (7 g) active dry yeast
- 3 cups (360 g) all-purpose flour
- 1 tsp (5 g) salt

Instructions:

1. **Prepare the Yeast Mixture:** In the bread machine pan, combine warm milk, vegetable oil, and sugar. Sprinkle yeast over and let sit for 5 minutes.
2. **Add Dry Ingredients:** Add flour and salt to the pan.
3. **Mix and Knead:** Select the **Dough** setting and press Start. The machine will mix and knead the dough.
4. **First Rise:** Let the dough rise in the pan for about 1 hour or until doubled in size.
5. **Shape and Second Rise:** Divide the dough into 8 portions, shape into buns, and place on a baking sheet. Let rise for another 30 minutes.
6. **Bake:** Bake at 375°F (190°C) for 15-20 minutes until golden brown.

Expert Tips:

- **Uniform Size:** Shape buns evenly for consistent cooking.
- **Cooling:** Cool on a wire rack to prevent sogginess.

11.5 Sandwich Bread Dough

Preparation Time:
10 minutes

Cooking Time:
1 hour

Total Time:
1 hour 10 minutes

Nutritional Information (per 1 oz serving):

Calories: 120
Protein: 4 g

Carbohydrates: 22 g
Fat: 2 g

Sodium: 220 mg
Sugars: 2 g

Bread Machine Setting: Basic

Quantity: 1 loaf

Ingredients:

- 1 cup (240 ml) warm water
- 1/4 cup (60 ml) vegetable oil

- 2 tbsp (30 g) sugar
- 2 1/4 tsp (7 g) active dry yeast

- 3 cups (360 g) all-purpose flour
- 1 tsp (5 g) salt

Instructions:

1. **Combine Ingredients:** In the bread machine pan, mix warm water, vegetable oil, and sugar. Sprinkle yeast over the top and let sit for 5 minutes.
2. **Add Dry Ingredients:** Add flour and salt to the pan.
3. **Mix and Knead:** Select the **Basic** setting and press Start. The machine will mix, knead, and rise the dough.
4. **Shape and Bake:** After the dough cycle is complete, shape into a loaf and place in a greased pan. Let rise for 30 minutes. Bake at 375°F (190°C) for 25-30 minutes.

Expert Tips:

- **Even Baking:** Ensure the dough is evenly shaped for uniform baking.
- **Cooling:** Allow the bread to cool completely before slicing to maintain texture.

11.6 Crackers Dough

Preparation Time:
10 minutes

Cooking Time:
30 minutes

Total Time:
40 minutes

Nutritional Information (per 1 oz serving):

Calories: 100

Carbohydrates: 14 g

Sodium: 180 mg

Protein: 2 g

Fat: 4 g

Sugars: 1 g

Bread Machine Setting: Dough

Quantity: 1 batch of crackers

Ingredients:

- 1 cup (120 g) all-purpose flour
- 1/2 cup (60 g) whole wheat flour
- 1/4 cup (60 ml) olive oil
- 1/4 cup (30 g) grated Parmesan cheese
- 1 tsp (5 g) salt
- 1/2 tsp (2 g) garlic powder
- 1/4 cup (60 ml) water

Instructions:

1. **Combine Ingredients:** In the bread machine pan, mix all ingredients except water. Slowly add water until a smooth dough forms.
2. **Mix and Knead:** Select the **Dough** setting and press Start. The machine will mix and knead the dough.
3. **Roll Out and Cut:** Roll out dough on a lightly floured surface to desired thickness. Cut into squares or desired shapes.

4. **Bake:** Place on a baking sheet and bake at 375°F (190°C) for 15-20 minutes or until golden and crisp.

Expert Tips:

- **Thinness:** Roll the dough as thin as possible for extra crispy crackers.
- **Even Baking:** Arrange crackers evenly on the baking sheet to ensure uniform baking.

11.7 Focaccia Dough

Preparation Time:	Cooking Time:	Total Time:
15 minutes	1 hour	1 hour 15 minutes

Nutritional Information (per 1 oz serving):

Calories: 150	**Carbohydrates:** 23 g	**Sodium:** 230 mg
Protein: 4 g	**Fat:** 6 g	**Sugars:** 1 g

Bread Machine Setting: Dough   **Quantity:** 1 focaccia

Ingredients:

- 1 1/2 cups (360 ml) warm water
- 1/4 cup (60 ml) olive oil
- 2 tsp (10 g) sugar
- 2 1/4 tsp (7 g) active dry yeast
- 4 cups (500 g) all-purpose flour
- 1 tbsp (15 g) salt
- 1/4 cup (60 g) chopped sun-dried tomatoes (optional)
- Fresh basil and sea salt for topping

Instructions:

1. **Prepare the Yeast Mixture:** In the bread machine pan, mix warm water, olive oil, and sugar. Sprinkle yeast over and let sit for 5 minutes.
2. **Add Dry Ingredients:** Add flour and salt to the pan. Mix until combined.
3. **Mix and Knead:** Select the **Dough** setting and press Start. The machine will mix and knead the dough.
4. **First Rise:** Let the dough rise in the pan for about 1 hour or until doubled.
5. **Shape and Bake:** Transfer to a greased baking sheet, dimple with your fingers, and top with sun-dried tomatoes, basil, and sea salt. Bake at 425°F (220°C) for 20-25 minutes.

Expert Tips:

- **Dimples:** Make deep dimples in the dough with your fingers for an authentic focaccia texture.
- **Toppings:** Customize with herbs and vegetables according to your taste.

Chapter 12: Special Occasion Breads

12.1 Festive Panettone

Preparation Time:
20 minutes

Cooking Time:
1 hour 30 minutes

Total Time:
1 hour 50 minutes

Nutritional Information (per 1 oz serving):

Calories: 150

Carbohydrates: 25 g

Sodium: 220 mg

Protein: 4 g

Fat: 5 g

Sugars: 10 g

Bread Machine Setting: Dough

Quantity: 1 panettone

Ingredients:

- 1/2 cup (120 ml) warm milk
- 1/2 cup (115 g) unsalted butter, softened
- 1/2 cup (100 g) sugar
- 3 large eggs
- 1/4 cup (60 ml) honey
- 2 1/4 tsp (7 g) active dry yeast
- 3 1/2 cups (420 g) all-purpose flour
- 1/2 cup (70 g) chopped candied fruit
- 1/2 cup (70 g) raisins
- 1/2 cup (60 g) chopped nuts
- 1 tsp (5 g) salt

Instructions:

1. **Prepare Yeast Mixture:** In the bread machine pan, combine warm milk, butter, and sugar. Sprinkle yeast over and let sit for 5 minutes.
2. **Add Ingredients:** Add eggs, honey, flour, and salt. Mix until well combined.
3. **Knead and Rise:** Select the **Dough** setting and press Start. After kneading, let the dough rise in the pan for 1 hour or until doubled in size.
4. **Add Fruit and Nuts:** Gently fold in candied fruit, raisins, and nuts.
5. **Shape and Rise:** Transfer the dough to a panettone mold. Let rise for another 30 minutes.
6. **Bake:** Bake at 350°F (175°C) for 50-60 minutes, or until a toothpick inserted into the center comes out clean.

Expert Tips:

- **Fruit Distribution:** Ensure even distribution of fruit and nuts for consistent flavor.
- **Cooling:** Allow to cool in the mold for 10 minutes before transferring to a wire rack.

12.2 Cupcake Bread

Preparation Time:
15 minutes

Cooking Time:
1 hour

Total Time:
1 hour 15 minutes

Nutritional Information (per 1 oz serving):

Calories: 140
Protein: 3 g

Carbohydrates: 22 g
Fat: 5 g

Sodium: 200 mg
Sugars: 7 g

Bread Machine Setting: Dough

Quantity: 1 loaf

Ingredients:

- 1 cup (240 ml) warm milk
- 1/4 cup (60 ml) vegetable oil
- 1/2 cup (100 g) sugar
- 2 large eggs

- 2 1/4 tsp (7 g) active dry yeast
- 3 cups (360 g) all-purpose flour
- 1 tsp (5 g) salt
- Sprinkles or icing for decoration

Instructions:

1. **Prepare Yeast Mixture:** In the bread machine pan, combine warm milk, vegetable oil, and sugar. Sprinkle yeast over and let sit for 5 minutes.
2. **Add Dry Ingredients:** Add eggs, flour, and salt.
3. **Mix and Knead:** Select the **Dough** setting and press Start. The machine will mix and knead the dough.
4. **Shape and Rise:** Transfer dough to a greased loaf pan and let rise for 30 minutes.
5. **Bake:** Bake at 375°F (190°C) for 25-30 minutes or until golden brown. Cool and decorate with sprinkles or icing.

Expert Tips:

- **Decoration:** Add sprinkles or icing after cooling for a festive touch.
- **Even Rising:** Ensure the dough is evenly spread in the pan for uniform baking.

12.3 Christmas Stollen

Preparation Time:
20 minutes

Cooking Time:
1 hour 15 minutes

Total Time:
1 hour 35 minutes

Nutritional Information (per 1 oz serving):

| **Calories:** 170 | **Carbohydrates:** 28 g | **Sodium:** 210 mg |
| **Protein:** 4 g | **Fat:** 6 g | **Sugars:** 10 g |

Bread Machine Setting: Dough   **Quantity:** 1 stollen

Ingredients:

- 1/2 cup (120 ml) warm milk
- 1/2 cup (115 g) unsalted butter, softened
- 1/2 cup (100 g) sugar
- 2 large eggs
- 1/4 cup (60 ml) rum (optional)
- 2 1/4 tsp (7 g) active dry yeast

- 3 1/2 cups (420 g) all-purpose flour
- 1/2 cup (70 g) chopped dried fruit
- 1/2 cup (70 g) chopped nuts
- 1/2 tsp (2.5 g) ground cinnamon
- 1/2 tsp (2.5 g) ground nutmeg
- 1/2 tsp (2.5 g) salt

Instructions:

1. **Prepare Yeast Mixture:** In the bread machine pan, mix warm milk, butter, and sugar. Sprinkle yeast over and let sit for 5 minutes.
2. **Add Ingredients:** Add eggs, rum, flour, spices, and salt.
3. **Mix and Knead:** Select the **Dough** setting and press Start. The machine will mix and knead the dough.
4. **Add Fruit and Nuts:** Gently fold in dried fruit and nuts.
5. **Shape and Rise:** Shape dough into a loaf and place on a baking sheet. Let rise for 45 minutes.
6. **Bake:** Bake at 350°F (175°C) for 45-50 minutes. Cool and dust with powdered sugar before serving.

Expert Tips:

- **Spices:** Adjust spices to taste for a more personalized flavor.
- **Storage:** Wrap tightly to keep fresh and moist.

12.4 Easter Bread

| **Preparation Time:** | **Cooking Time:** | **Total Time:** |
| 20 minutes | 1 hour | 1 hour 20 minutes |

Nutritional Information (per 1 oz serving):

| **Calories:** 140 | **Carbohydrates:** 22 g | **Sodium:** 200 mg |
| **Protein:** 4 g | **Fat:** 4 g | **Sugars:** 6 g |

Bread Machine Setting: Dough   **Quantity:** 1 loaf

Ingredients:

- 1 cup (240 ml) warm milk
- 1/4 cup (60 ml) vegetable oil
- 1/2 cup (100 g) sugar
- 2 large eggs

- 2 1/4 tsp (7 g) active dry yeast
- 3 cups (360 g) all-purpose flour
- 1 tsp (5 g) salt
- Colored sugar or icing for decoration

Instructions:

1. **Prepare Yeast Mixture:** In the bread machine pan, combine warm milk, vegetable oil, and sugar. Sprinkle yeast over and let sit for 5 minutes.
2. **Add Dry Ingredients:** Add eggs, flour, and salt.
3. **Mix and Knead:** Select the **Dough** setting and press Start. The machine will mix and knead the dough.
4. **Shape and Rise:** Transfer dough to a greased loaf pan and let rise for 30 minutes.
5. **Bake:** Bake at 375°F (190°C) for 25-30 minutes. Cool and decorate with colored sugar or icing.

Expert Tips:

- **Decoration:** Use colored sugar or icing to make the bread festive.
- **Consistency:** Ensure dough is well-risen before baking for a light texture.

12.5 Themed Brioche

Preparation Time:	Cooking Time:	Total Time:
20 minutes	1 hour 30 minutes	1 hour 50 minutes

Nutritional Information (per 1 oz serving):

Calories: 180	Carbohydrates: 24 g	Sodium: 210 mg
Protein: 5 g	Fat: 8 g	Sugars: 7 g

Bread Machine Setting: Dough   **Quantity:** 1 loaf

Ingredients:

- 1 cup (240 ml) warm milk
- 1/2 cup (115 g) unsalted butter, softened
- 1/2 cup (100 g) sugar

- 4 large eggs
- 3 cups (360 g) all-purpose flour
- 1/4 cup (30 g) vital wheat gluten
- 2 1/4 tsp (7 g) active dry yeast

- 1 tsp (5 g) salt
- Optional: chocolate chips, fruit, or nuts for customization

Instructions:

1. **Prepare Yeast Mixture:** In the bread machine pan, mix warm milk, butter, and sugar. Add yeast and let sit for 5 minutes.
2. **Add Dry Ingredients:** Add eggs, flour, vital wheat gluten, and salt.
3. **Mix and Knead:** Select the **Dough** setting and press Start. The machine will mix and knead the dough.
4. **Customize:** Fold in chocolate chips, fruit, or nuts if desired.
5. **Shape and Rise:** Transfer dough to a greased loaf pan and let rise for 1 hour.
6. **Bake:** Bake at 350°F (175°C) for 45-50 minutes. Cool before serving.

Expert Tips:

- **Add-ins:** Customize with your favorite add-ins for a personalized touch.
- **Rising:** Ensure dough is well-risen before baking for a light texture.

12.6 BBQ Buns

Preparation Time:
15 minutes

Cooking Time:
1 hour

Total Time:
1 hour 15 minutes

Nutritional Information (per 1 oz serving):

Calories: 130
Protein: 4 g

Carbohydrates: 22 g
Fat: 3 g

Sodium: 190 mg
Sugars: 5 g

Bread Machine Setting: Dough

Quantity: 8 buns

Ingredients:

- 1 cup (240 ml) warm water
- 1/4 cup (60 ml) vegetable oil
- 1/4 cup (50 g) sugar
- 2 1/4 tsp (7 g) active dry yeast
- 3 cups (360 g) all-purpose flour
- 1 tsp (5 g) salt

Instructions:

1. **Prepare Yeast Mixture:** In the bread machine pan, combine warm water, vegetable oil, and sugar. Sprinkle yeast over and let sit for 5 minutes.
2. **Add Dry Ingredients:** Add flour and salt.
3. **Mix and Knead:** Select the **Dough** setting and press Start. The machine will mix and knead the dough.
4. **Shape and Rise:** Divide dough into 8 equal portions and shape into buns. Place on a greased baking sheet and let rise for 30 minutes.
5. **Bake:** Bake at 375°F (190°C) for 15-20 minutes or until golden brown. Cool before serving.

Expert Tips:

- **Uniform Size:** Ensure buns are evenly sized for uniform baking.
- **Cooling:** Allow to cool slightly before serving to maintain softness.

12.7 Energy Bread

Preparation Time:	**Cooking Time:**	**Total Time:**
15 minutes	1 hour	1 hour 15 minutes

Nutritional Information (per 1 oz serving):

Calories: 180	**Carbohydrates:** 20 g	**Sodium:** 220 mg
Protein: 8 g	**Fat:** 6 g	**Sugars:** 3 g

Bread Machine Setting: Dough   **Quantity:** 1 loaf

Ingredients:

- 1 cup (240 ml) warm water
- 1/2 cup (120 ml) Greek yogurt
- 1/4 cup (60 ml) honey
- 1/4 cup (60 ml) vegetable oil
- 2 1/4 tsp (7 g) active dry yeast
- 1 1/2 cups (180 g) whole wheat flour
- 1 1/2 cups (180 g) all-purpose flour
- 1/2 cup (60 g) protein powder
- 1 tsp (5 g) salt

Instructions:

1. **Prepare Yeast Mixture:** In the bread machine pan, mix warm water, Greek yogurt, and honey. Sprinkle yeast over and let sit for 5 minutes.
2. **Add Dry Ingredients:** Add whole wheat flour, all-purpose flour, protein powder, and salt.
3. **Mix and Knead:** Select the **Dough** setting and press Start. The machine will mix and knead the dough.
4. **Shape and Rise:** Transfer dough to a greased loaf pan and let rise for 30 minutes.
5. **Bake:** Bake at 375°F (190°C) for 25-30 minutes. Cool before slicing.

Expert Tips:

- **Protein Boost:** Adjust protein powder to increase energy content.
- **Even Baking:** Ensure dough is evenly distributed in the pan for uniform baking.

Adjusting for Different Loaf Sizes

Bread machines typically bake loaves of 1 lb, 1.5 lb, or 2 lb. Here's how to adjust ingredient quantities:

1. **For a 1 lb loaf:** Use 67% of the ingredients from the standard recipe.
2. **For a 1.5 lb loaf:** Use the full recipe (100% of ingredients).
3. **For a 2 lb loaf:** Increase ingredients by 33%.

This method ensures that your bread rises and bakes perfectly, regardless of loaf size.

Here's an example of how to adjust ingredients for different loaf sizes:

Let's say your standard recipe for a 1.5 lb loaf calls for:

- 3 cups (360 g) bread flour
- 1 cup (240 ml) water
- 1 1/2 tsp (7 g) salt

For a 1 lb loaf (67%):

- 2 cups (240 g) bread flour
- 2/3 cup (160 ml) water
- 1 tsp (4.7 g) salt

For a 2 lb loaf (133%):

- 4 cups (480 g) bread flour
- 1 1/3 cup (320 ml) water
- 2 tsp (9.3 g) salt

This method helps you scale the recipe easily!

Here's a simple way to calculate ingredient adjustments for different loaf sizes:

Formula:

For a 1 lb loaf:
Ingredient Amount×0.67

For a 2 lb loaf:
Ingredient Amount×1.33

Example:
If your recipe calls for 3 cups of flour for a 1.5 lb loaf:

For a 1 lb loaf:
3 cups×0.67=2 cups

For a 2 lb loaf:
3 cups×1.33=4 cups

Use this formula to easily adjust any ingredient in your recipes!

5 BONUS

CHRISTMAS AND

NEW YEAR'S EDITION

Julia Smith